BALLPARKS

Previous page: Looking toward Fenway Park's diamond in the 1950s. The "Green Monster" is on the right.
National Baseball Hall of Fame

Above: Fireworks at Oakland Coliseum during the singing of national anthem on opening night in 1998.
San Francisco Chronicle

BALLPARKS

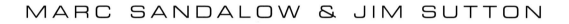

MARC SANDALOW & JIM SUTTON

CHARTWELL
BOOKS, INC.

This edition published by

CHARTWELL BOOKS, INC.
A Division of
BOOK SALES, INC.
114 Northfield Avenue
Edison, New Jersey 08837

ISBN-13: 978-0-7858-2463-3
ISBN-10: 0-7858-2463-4

© 2008 by Compendium Publishing Ltd, 43 Frith Street,
Soho, London, W1D 4SA, United Kingdom

From an idea proposed by Frank Oppel

Cataloging-in-Publication data is available from the Library
of Congress

Printed and bound in China

Design: Tony Stocks@Compendium

Photographs
All images are credited with their captions. Photos came
from Getty Images, Corbis, the Baseball Hall of Fame,
Digitalballparks.com, Roger Miller, and the San Francisco
Chronicle: thanks to all those who helped.

Right: Workmen from the
Wrigley Field grounds crew
shovel snow from the infield
of the park on April 7, 2003.
The Chicago Cubs were to
play their home opener
against the Montreal Expos
but the game was cancelled
due to the snow.
Getty Images

CONTENTS

INTRODUCTION

Baseball is unique among American sports. Football, basketball, and hockey are played on identical fields, courts, and rinks. Only in baseball does the park define the game.

There is simply no feeling like walking into a ballpark on an early spring day and taking in the expanse of lush, green, meticulously groomed, and mostly uninhabited grass. There is a buzz, a smell, and an excitement to a baseball stadium that cannot be recreated on the evening news or the morning's sports pages, as dutifully as they try.

The Green Monster in Boston, the ivy in Chicago, the center field hill in Houston, the Bermuda Triangle in Miami, the convertible roof in Seattle, the baggy in Minneapolis, and the cove in San Francisco: these not only brand each park with a distinct appearance, they change the way the game is played.

There is little discussion of how many baskets Wilt Chamberlain would have shot, or how many goals Wayne Gretsky would have scored, had they spent their careers at the Boston Garden. Yet baseball fans can spend hours debating what Babe Ruth might have done as a Fenway slugger; how many home runs Willie Mays might have hit if not for the wind at Candlestick Park; or whether the Minnesota Twins would have won a world championship, let alone two, if not for the helpful horrors of their Metrodome. A game at Wrigley Field in Chicago is a very different experience than one at Dodger Stadium in Los Angeles, Pro Player in Miami, or Shea Stadium in New York.

This book tries to highlight those differences. It is not an authoritative account of baseball stadiums, or a encyclopedic telling of their history. Instead, it is a picture-filled look at what makes the current major league parks, and some of the famous old ones, so special.

To anyone trying to write about ballparks, it is quickly apparent that parks are in a perpetual state of change. Since Baltimore Memorial Stadium opened in 1954, 38 new ballparks have been constructed (about one every 16 months), several of which have already been replaced and demolished. As this book was being researched, two ballparks changed their names, and two others shut their doors to make way for new ones. By next season, many of the parks described in this book will have undergone some renovations. To a baseball fan, the changes provide a fascinating glimpse at the game's evolution.

The quirkiness and intimacy of the turn-of-the-century ballparks was largely the product of geography and finances, as team owners tried to cram stadiums into small urban lots, in places where fans would be plentiful. If the lot was misshaped, as at Washington's Griffith Stadium (where one home owner refused to budge from the stadium site), the crooked outfield wall was simply built around it. Fenway's Green Monster was erected because of the park's tight quarters, and to block residents on Lansdowne Street from getting a free look at the game. Such quirks are now carefully added to stadium designs, sometimes at great additional cost, to capture a sense of history and tradition.

Today, it is also an article of faith among baseball owners that stadiums should be intimate and small, built to boost home run totals to lure fans to the games. Yet in 1910, when Charlie Comiskey built a park on the south side of Chicago for his White Sox, he wanted a huge outfield, partly for the thrill of watching fielders make long sprints for balls, and for the excitement of watching runners try for extra base hits, rather than lope around the bases in a lazy home run trot.

A generation from now, the game will have evolved again. Perhaps the short fences that mark early 21st century parks will seem like dinosaurs. Just as the opening of steel-and-concrete Shibe Park in Philadelphia in 1909 and the opening of Oriole Park at Camden Yards in Baltimore in 1992 touched off revolutions in ballpark designs, it is easy to imagine some future innovation changing the look of baseball stadiums.

Some qualities seem certain to endure. The perfect diamond, the lush turf, the intimacy between the players and the fans, the geographic landmarks that let you know exactly where the game is being played. For 30 major league cities, there are few structures that better tell their story than their ballpark.

The historian Jacques Barzun famously wrote: "Whoever wants to know the heart and mind of

Fans are what it's all about. Will this new generation of Cubs' fans still be visiting Wrigley Field with their children? Victor Ireland, Jacob Peckerson, and Sinhue Mendoda show their loyalty to the Cubs before the game against the Florida Marlins, October 7, 2003.
Photo by Brian Bahr/Getty Images

America, had better learn baseball." In a similar vein, whoever wants to know baseball had better learn ballparks. This book is a start.

Acknowledgments

Everyone has an opinion about ballparks. Thanks to Vernard Atkins, Zac Coile, Bob Congdon, Bonnie DeSimone, Ed Epstein, Carl Nolte, Marcie Sandalow, and Ellen Loerke for sharing their insightful views with us. Special thanks to Tom McClurg for his careful reading of the text and his constant reminder of what makes baseball great.

Many people helped us in the hunt for photos. Special thanks to W.C. Burdick of the National Baseball Hall of Fame, Marc Seigerman at Getty Images, Gary Fong at the *San Francisco Chronicle*, Tony Pastore of Digital Ballparks.com, Rob Arra of Everlasting Images, and Roger Miller of Baltimore's Roger Miller Studio. Ltd.

And special thanks to Sandra Forty, an English girl who really knows how to find photos of American ballparks, even if she doesn't know much about the games that are played in them.

Thank you, every one and all.

Exterior view of Camden Yards late in the afternoon of August 15, 2003, during the game between the Orioles and the Yankees. The Yankees won 6–4.
Photo by Jerry Driendl/Getty Images

THE AMERICAN LEAGUE

The roster of American League cities sounds like a refrain from a Chuck Berry song: Detroit, Chicago, Baltimore, Boston, and K.C. When it was founded in 1901, the American League was the junior circuit, coming to life a quarter of a century after the National League, and bringing professional baseball to America's thriving metropolises. Of the eight original American League cities, only Washington, the nation's capital, is now without a professional team.

Some American League teams have come and gone, such as the Boston Pilgrims, the Cleveland Naps, the Seattle Pilots, and the Washington Senators. Roughly 50 stadiums have been home to American League teams. Several of the old classics—Detroit's Tiger Stadium, Cleveland's Municipal Stadium, and Chicago's Comiskey Park—closed in the 1990s.

The American League's oldest stadium is Fenway Park, which opened the same week the

Titanic sank in 1912. Exactly 80 years later, Baltimore's Camden Yards sparked a new wave of classic-style parks, structures which sought to imitate the intimacy of Fenway and other older parks. There is now talk of a new ballpark in Minnesota, hope in Oakland, and—to the horror of some Bostonians—even a discussion of how to rebuild Fenway. However the last stadium built for an American League team was Detroit's Comerica Park in 2000.

Fenway Park seen from inside the Boston Red Sox dugout during the game against the Yankees on July 25, 2003. The Yankees won 4–3.
Photo by Jerry Driendl/Getty Images

11

AMERICAN LEAGUE EAST

The American League's Eastern Division boasts some of baseball's most storied parks.

Fenway Park is where Babe Ruth began his career, and Yankee Stadium is where he reached power-hitting immortality. Ty Cobb, Walter Johnson, Hank Greenberg, Jimmy Foxx, Tris Speaker, each played on the very fields where Red Sox and Yankees still play. Fans still stream into the South Bronx park where Lou Gehrig bid baseball adieu and sit in the same Boston bleachers where Ted Williams hit his longest shot.

To the north, SkyDome with its convertible roof, showed the sporting world how to handle the elements. Orioles Park at Camden Yard reminded fans of the game's intrinsic beauty, while Tropicana Field in Florida jammed about as much entertainment as can fit inside a structure built for baseball.

There is talk of remodeling Fenway to meet 21st century standards. However the parks of the American League Eastern Division largely look like they are here to stay.

Right: Oriole Park at Camden Yards during the game between the Orioles and the Yankees on August 14, 2003. The Yankees won 4–3.
Photo by Jerry Driendl/Getty Images

BALTIMORE ORIOLES

ORIOLE PARK AT CAMDEN YARDS

BALTIMORE ORIOLES

Address:
333 West Camden Street
Baltimore, MD 21201
Capacity: 48,876
Opening day: April 6, 1992—Baltimore Orioles 2, Cleveland Indians 0
Cost to construct: $110 million
Architect: HOK Sports
Dimensions (ft):
Left Field—333
Left Center—364
Center Field—410
Right Center—373
Right Field—318
Defining feature: B&O Warehouse in right field
Little-known ground rule: Fly ball hitting the grounds crew shed roof in right field and bouncing back into play: Home Run
Most expensive seat: $45
Cheapest seat: $8
World Series: None
All-Star Game: 1993

Memorable moments:
1993 July 13—Seattle's Ken Griffey Jr. becomes the first player to hit the B&O warehouse on a fly, during a home run contest preceding the All-Star game.
1995 September 6—Cal Ripken Jr. smacks a fourth-inning home run while playing in his 2131st consecutive game, surpassing Lou Gehrig as baseball's "Iron Man."
1996 September 6—Eddie Murray hits his 500th home run.

The opening of Oriole Park at Camden Yards touched off a baseball revolution. After three decades of constructing cookie-cutter coliseums, Baltimore reintroduced the concept of a ballpark. Nestled beside train lines in the city's inner harbor, the yard was a throwback to the days of Babe Ruth, who had been born just two blocks away. Its brick facade, asymmetrical outfield, panoramic view of downtown Baltimore, and the imposing B&O warehouse—which taunts left handed hitters—reminded Americans why baseball was long regarded as the national pastime.

The rest of the baseball world took notice. Within a decade, ballparks in Cleveland, Denver, Pittsburgh, San Francisco, Arlington, Seattle, Atlanta, Milwaukee, Houston, Detroit, and San Diego would mimic Baltimore's old-time appeal. Baseball history guided the architects, who were influenced by Ebbets Field (Brooklyn), Shibe Park (Philadelphia), Fenway Park (Boston), Crosley Field (Cincinnati), Forbes Field (Pittsburgh), Wrigley Field (Chicago), and the Polo Grounds (New York). The cozy dimensions, the steel trusses, the rustic clock on the center field scoreboard, all gave the park a classic feel.

But the park is new. It has luxury boxes (a major revenue source), microbrews, a family picnic area, and shiny bronze baseballs imbedded in Eutaw Street, which runs between the warehouse and the outfield bleachers. Just beyond the bleachers, fans can buy barbeque made by Oriole great Boog Powell, who can sometimes be found signing hot dog wrappers and ticket stubs.

The history is more than just appearance. Ruth's father owned a tavern about where center field now sits. The eight-story, red-bricked, turn of the century B&O warehouse, the park's defining feature, is more than 1,000 feet long, built in 1895 to handle long railroad freight cars, and is said to be the longest building on the East Coast. It sits 432 feet away from home plate and though Ken Griffey Jr. reached it during a home run competition before the 1993 All-Star Game, no one has yet done so during a game. The park's anchor in a revitalized downtown was a big reason that the legislature agreed to help pay for it with the sale of lottery tickets. When it was built, Maryland Governor William Donald Schaefer called the ballpark "the largest single economic development opportunity we have had in the last decade," and its success spurred other clubs to look beyond land-rich suburban areas for their stadium homes.

The move from Baltimore's old Memorial Stadium to Camden Yards "is like coming from the slums to a palace," Orioles' outfield David Segui said the week the park opened. "If we play half as good as this place looks we'll be pretty good this year."

Unfortunately for O's fans, the park has fared better than the Orioles who are still looking to bring a World Series to Camden Yards.

Above: Eutaw Street outside Camden Yards thronging with fans before a game.
Digitalballparks.com

Right: A sculpture of Babe Ruth stands tall outside Oriole Park at Camden Yards. George Herman "Babe" Ruth (1895–1948) was born in Baltimore but started his long career in 1914 with the Boston Red Sox. It was with the Yankees 1920–34 that he came to the fore with prodigious batting feats-54 home runs, then a record, in 1920; 60 in 1927. Among the greatest players baseball has ever seen, he played in 10 World Series, hit 714 home runs (a record that stood until 1974), and was elected to the Hall of Fame in 1936.
Photo by Jerry Driendl/Getty Images

Night panorama of Oriole Park.
Photo by Jerry Driendl/Getty Images

Left and Above: Night falls over Baltimore and Oriole Park in this 2003 photograph, the out-of-town scoreboard lighting up in the fading light. Babe Ruth was born two blocks from the ballpark 75 years before Oriole Park opened in 1992. The long building past right field is a remnant from the days of the "B&O"—the Baltimore & Ohio Railroad. Built at the turn of the century the warehouse is 1,016 feet long and is used today to house the Orioles' management offices as well as restaurants and bars. Much of the success of the new park has been attributed to its location in the midst of Baltimore's bustling inner harbor.
Photos by Roger Miller

Right: Bleachers and scoreboard from right field: note the B&O warehouse at right and the Emerson Bromo-Seltzer Tower in the distance. Listed on the National Register of Historic Places, the Bromo-Seltzer Tower was modeled after the Palazzo Vecchio in Florence, Italy. It was completed in 1911 and has been a Baltimore landmark ever since. It was built by Captain Isaac Emerson, the inventor of Bromo-Seltzer.
Digitalballparks.com

Left: Pre-game introduction of the home team on April 6, 1992, the first home game of the season for the Orioles and the first official game played at Oriole Park at Camden Yards. A capacity crowd of more than 48,000 enjoyed a beautiful day at the new ballpark and a victory celebration as the Orioles beat the Cleveland Indians, 2–0.
Photo by Roger Miller

Right: The outside of Camden Yards from the parking lot.
Digitalballparks.com

Left: Spectators outside Oriole Park's oldest feature, the B&O warehouse. Oriole Park is a popular location, with average attendances of over 40,000 and a capacity of 48,000.

Photo by: Roger Miller

Above and Right: Aerial views of Memorial Stadium, the home of the Orioles until replaced by the new Oriole Park at Camden Yards in 1992. Fans who had loudly voiced their dissatisfaction over the change were soon silenced by the easy access the downtown location provided and the sheer pleasure of watching a game at the new ballpark.
Photos by: Roger Miller

Left: The "Memorial Wall" at Memorial Stadium was a very large and visible concrete plaque located on the outside of the ballpark behind home plate. Its inscription read: "Dedicated as a memorial to all who so valiantly fought in the world wars with eternal gratitude to those who made the supreme sacrifice to preserve equality and freedom throughout the world—time will not dim the glory of their deeds." Before the stadium was demolished in February 2001, the wall was dismantled and preserved. Parts of it have been incorporated into a new Veteran's Memorial at Oriole Park at Camden Yards.
Photo: by Roger Miller

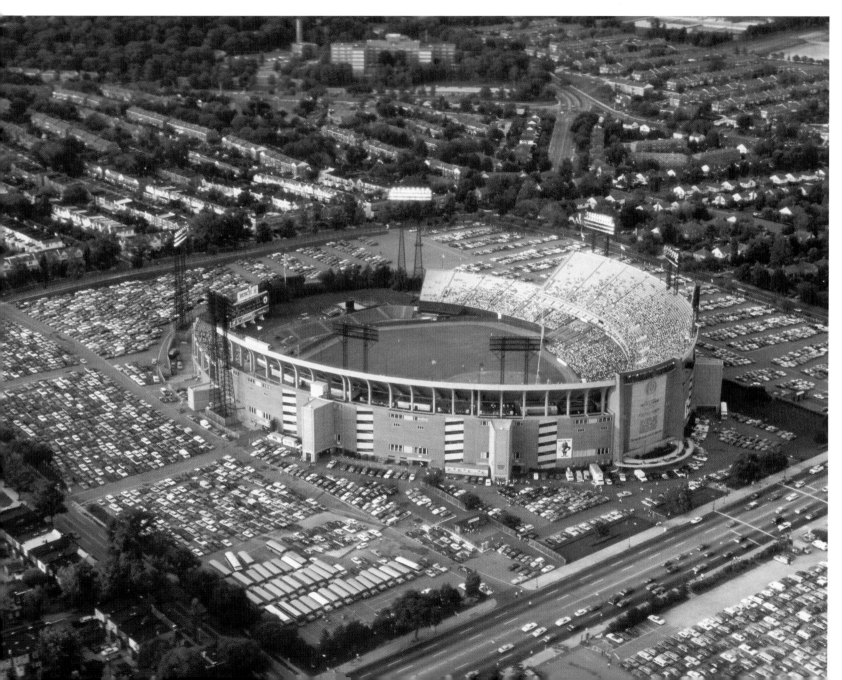

MEMORIAL STADIUM (1954–91)

Home of the Baltimore Orioles

Memorial Stadium, like the city it served, was a no frills place to watch baseball. Originally built for minor league baseball and professional football, an uncovered second deck was added in 1954, when the Browns moved to Baltimore from St. Louis and became the Orioles. Vice President Richard Nixon threw out the ceremonial first pitch on the park's opening day. The park was best known for its meticulous field and devoted fans, many of whom sneered at plans in the early 1990s to replace the worn stadium with a downtown park.

Memorial Stadium was home to Brooks Robinson and Frank Robinson, where Jim Palmer, Dave McNally, Pat Dobson, and Mike Cuellar each won 20 games in the same year (1971), where Cal Ripken's iron man streak began, and where Earl Weaver's umpire-arguing, three-run-home-run style of baseball produced champions.

BOSTON RED SOX

FENWAY PARK

BOSTON RED SOX

Address:
4 Yawkey Way
Boston, MA 02215
Capacity: 33,871
Opening day: April 20, 1912—Boston Red Sox 7,
New York Highlanders 6 (11 innings)
Cost to construct: $650,000
Architect: Osborne Engineering Company
Dimensions (ft):
Left Field—310
Left Center—390
Center Field—420
Right Center—380
Right Field—302
Defining feature: Green Monster
Little-known ground rule: A ball going through the
Green Monster scoreboard, either on the bound or fly,
is two bases
Most expensive seat: $70
Cheapest seat: $10
World Series: 1912, 1914, 1918, 1946, 1967, 1975, 1986
All-Star Game: 1946, 1961, 1999

Memorable moments:
1914 July 11—Babe Ruth earns a victory as a pitcher in
his major league debut.
1918 September 11—Red Sox win the World Series
over the Chicago Cubs.
1948 May 12—Red Sox games televised for first time
on WBZ-TV.
1960 September 28—Ted Williams hits a home run in
his final at-bat.
1975 October 21—Carton Fisk hits a 12th-inning home
run off the left field foul pole to win game six of
the World Series against the Cincinnati Reds.
1978 October 2—Yankee shortstop Bucky Dent hits a
seventh-inning home run over the Green Monster
to lead the Yankees to an AL East championship in
a single-game playoff.
1986 April 29—Roger Clemens strikes out 20
Mariners.

The Great Wall of China. The Wailing Wall in Jerusalem. The Green Monster in Fenway Park. Few structures in architecture, and none in baseball, are more identifiable than the 37-foot wall that separates Lansdowne Street from the outfield where Duffy Lewis, Ted Williams, and Carl Yazstremski once roamed.

A billboard for the greatness of baseball, the original wall, just 25 feet high, was probably built to keep residents in neighboring apartments from sneaking a free peak at the game. The Green Monster was expanded to its current height in 1934 and painted green in 1947. The seats built on top in 2003 have become among the most prized in baseball.

Fenway, the oldest of today's major league parks, is a living monument to baseball history. Babe Ruth's early pitching days, the Red Sox' dramatic—and final—World Series triumph in 1918, Jimmy Foxx and Ted Williams' slugging, Tony Conigliaro's beaning, Carl Yazstremski's left field mastery, Jim Rice's power, and Pedro Martinez's dominance, make it more than a

"little lyrical bandbox of a ballpark," as John Updike famously described it.

Constructed in time for the 1912 season, the new ballpark was named by then Red Sox owner John I. Taylor because it was built in a marshy area of Boston known as the Fens. The opening was pushed off the front pages of Boston newspapers because of the *Titanic*, which had sunk just six days earlier. Mayor John F. Fitzgerald threw out the first pitch at the ceremony marking the park's opening, 48 years before his yet-to-be born grandson, John Fitzgerald Kennedy would win the presidency.

Before the Green Monster there was a steep mound of dirt that rose 10 feet to the left field wall, a fielding nightmare played so masterfully by Red Sox left fielder Duffy Lewis it was nicknamed "Duffy's Cliff." Fire has repeatedly reshaped baseball's most distinctive park. In 1926, the wooden bleachers along the left field line burned down, creating an opening that provided fielders a chance to catch foul balls outside the grandstand. Another fire in 1934 convinced the owners to replace wooden stands with

concrete. It was post-World War II fire regulations that made the park's capacity, which once approached 48,000, shrink to the lowest of any park in the majors.

In a time-honored tradition, the park was also shaped to fit its talent. The bullpens were moved to right field in the 1940s to shorten the fences and take advantage of Williams' left-handed power. A bright red seat in the right field bleachers (Section 42, Row 37, Seat 21) marks the spot of Williams' longest Fenway blast, a 502-foot shot on June 9, 1946, off Fred Hutchinson of the Detroit Tigers. While balls fly over the Green Monster in left with regularity (a 23-foot tall screen was installed above the left field wall to protect windows across Lansdowne Street in 1936), no player has ever hit a home run over the right-field roof.

Today, the base of the left field wall is anchored by a manual scoreboard, which not only updates American League scores with 16-inch-high numbers (National League scores are electronic) but features two vertical strips which spell out the initials of former team owners Tom

Yawkey and Jean Yawkey—TAY and JRY—in Morse code.

Fenway has been around for most of baseball's history. However it has not witnessed a Red Sox world championship since its infancy. On the afternoon of September 11, 1918, Les Mann, the Chicago Cubs leftfielder, tapped a ground ball to Sox second baseman Dave Shean, who tossed over to Stuffy McInnis for the out and a 2 to 1 victory. More than eight decades and 7,000 games later, Fenway has yet to celebrate another World Series triumph.

Right: Postwar aerial view of Fenway Park before the extensive modifications to the stands. Note no bleachers on top of the Green Monster; these were added before the 2003 season.
National Baseball Hall of Fame

Left: A view outside Fenway Park as fans arrive for the game between the Red Sox and the Yankees on July 25, 2003. The Yankees won 4–3.
Photo by: Jerry Driendl/Getty Images

Right: Panoramic interior view of Fenway Park from the seats above first base during the July 25, 2003 Red Sox-Yankees game. Note the bleachers atop the Green Monster.
Photo by: Jerry Driendl/Getty Images

Right: Mounted police on crowd control outside Fenway Park in 1912.
National Baseball Hall of Fame

Far Right: A complementary pair to the last photograph. This one, some 40 years later, is a postwar view of Fenway Park that shows clearly some of the building that had taken place since 1912.
National Baseball Hall of Fame

NEW YORK YANKEES

YANKEE STADIUM

NEW YORK YANKEES

Address:
East 161st Street at River Ave.
Bronx, NY 10451
Capacity: 57,545
Opening day: April 18, 1923—New York Yankees 4, Boston
Red Sox 1
Cost to construct: $2.5 million
Architect: Osborn Engineering (1923); Praeger-Kavanaugh-
Waterbury (1976)
Dimensions (ft):
Left Field—318
Left Center—399
Center Field—408
Right Center—385
Right Field—314
Defining feature: Monument Park
Little-known ground rule: A ball hitting the foul pole in the
1930s was in play, not a homer
Most expensive seat: $80
Cheapest seat: $10
World Series: 1923, 1926–28, 1932, 1936–39, 1941–43, 1947,
1949–53, 1955–58, 1960–64, 1976–78, 1981, 1996,
1998–2001, 2003
All-Star Game: 1939, 1960, 1977

Memorable moments:
1923 April 18—Babe Ruth hits a three-run homer against
Boston Red Sox in stadium's first game.
1925 June 1—Lou Gehrig begins a 2,130-consecutive game
streak, pinch hitting for Pee Wee Wanniger.
1927 September 30—Babe Ruth hits his 60th home run on
the season's final day
1939 July 4—Lou Gehrig's No. 4 is the first number retired in
baseball. Gehrig tells the adoring crowd: "Today I consider
myself the luckiest man on the face of the earth."
1961 October 1—Roger Maris hits his 61st home run in the
season's final game.
2001 November 1—Scott Brosius hits a two-out, two-run
home run to lead the Yankees to a ninth inning World
Series comeback against the Arizona Diamondbacks for a
second consecutive night.

Few structures house more American memories than Yankee Stadium. Ruth, Gehrig, DiMaggio, and Mantle are among the legends that have made history on these 10 acres in the South Bronx. Opened during the Harding presidency and still filling seats 13 presidents later, the majestic, triple-decked structure has hosted heavyweight championships, fabled football games, international soccer matches, world leaders, two popes, Bruce Springsteen, and Pink Floyd.

Yankee Stadium is synonymous with the most successful sports franchise in America, hosting the World Series, on average, nearly every other year since it opened.

America was dotted with ballparks in 1923, when the Yankees opened the first baseball field to be dubbed a "stadium." Like the team that called it home, there was nothing modest or understated about its confines. Three decks of grandstands, originally intended to encircle the park to deprive non-paying bystanders a free look, rose above home plate, with a distinctive copper frieze decorating the roof of the top deck.

Babe Ruth himself, a left-handed hitter who is responsible for the short right field porch, hit the park's first home run to the roaring approval of the New York faithful, who quickly called it "the house that Ruth built."

It was here, just across the Harlem River from the Polo Grounds (which the Giants and even the Yankees once called home), that Joe McCarthy and Casey Stengel managed the Yankees to a combined 18 pennants, where Ruth hit his 60th and where Roger Maris hit No. 61. It was the home to Murderer's row, the Iron Horse, the Yankee Clipper, and the "Straw that stirs the drink."

Cemetery-sized monuments to Manager Miller Huggins and later Gehrig and Ruth were placed in deep center field, 10 feet from the wall. Patrons could pay homage to their heroes as they exited through the center field gate, and watch as balls hit sharply to center field occasionally rattled around gravestone-looking monuments. Plaques to DiMaggio and Mantle were added in 1969.

The legends were not limited to baseball. It was here on a cold November day in 1928, that Notre Dame coach Knute Rockne, facing an undefeated Army team, asked his players to "win one for the Gipper," which they did on a pair of second half touchdowns. It was here that the Baltimore Colts defeated the New York Giants in sudden death during the 1958 NFL championship, regarded as "the greatest game ever played." Joe Louis claimed the heavyweight championship of the world here. Pele scored goals. Pope Paul VI delivered mass in 1965, and Pope John Paul II did the same 14 years later.

Decades of use necessitated major renovations, and for the 1974 and 1975 seasons the Yankees played at Shea Stadium as their stadium underwent reconstruction costing at least 25 times more than the original park. The new stadium met mixed reviews. The copper frieze was replaced by plastic, the monuments in center field were moved beyond the outfield walls. Some complained that a baseball relic had been turned into another cookie-cutter design.

Nevertheless, a park built before the Depression had been remodeled to last into the 21st century. The pillars that obstructed some views were gone. Luxury boxes were added.

Fans can now visit the monuments—which include tributes to McCarthy, Stengel, Thurman Munson, Elston Howard, and Roger Maris among others—before games.

The legends continued to grow in the new park. In a 1996 league championship game against Baltimore, 12-year-old fan Jeffrey Maier reached over his right field seat and caught Derek Jeter's fly ball, giving the Yanks a home run that wasn't, and leading to an eleventh-inning Yankee victory. A succession of dramatic come-from-behind World Series victories added to the stadium's mystique. And just two weeks after the September 11, 2001, terrorist attacks, Yankee Stadium hosted a nationally televised "Prayer for America" to honor those who had survived, and pay respect to those who hadn't.

Left: Taken on Yankee Stadium's opening day, this photograph shows Jacob Ruppert, Jr.—the "Colonel"—an important NYC brewer and philanthropist, next to Kenesaw Mountain Landis (right)—baseball's first commissioner who was elected to office in 1920.
National Baseball Hall of Fame

Below: The outside of Yankee Stadium on opening day, April 18, 1923. It hosted nearly 75,000 fans.
National Baseball Hall of Fame

Right: View from inside the stands over right field toward the diamond. Note the decorative cast-iron work on the roof edge. Photo taken in 1947 during the World Series between the Yankees and the Dodgers.
Associated Press/National Baseball Hall of Fame

Far right: A panoramic view of the baseball diamond taken during a game between the Texas Rangers and the Yankees on April 12, 2000. The Yankees defeated the Rangers 8–6.
Photo by Al Bello/Allsport via Getty Images

Left: Yankee Stadium during the Mets-Yankees game on June 27, 2003. The Yankees won 6-4.
Photo by: Jerry Driendl/Getty Images

Following page, Left: Another view of Yankee Stadium during the game against the Texas Rangers on April 12, 2000.
Photo by Al Bello/Allsport via Getty Images

Following page, Right: An exterior view of Yankee Stadium and its proud declaration of 26 World Championships. The structure in the shape of a baseball bat was erected in front of the stadium in 1976. For fans, it's a popular meeting point. Its real function is to serve as an exhaust chimney for the stadium's boilers. The design is modeled after a Louisville Slugger, just like that used by Yankee Sluggers to win those 26 World Championships.
National Baseball Hall of Fame

Left: Yankee Stadium from first base lower level during the Mets-Yankees on June 28,. The Yankees won 7-1. *Photo by: Jerry Driendl/Getty Images*

TAMPA BAY DEVIL RAYS

TROPICANA FIELD

TAMPA BAY DEVIL RAYS

Address:
One Tropicana Drive
St. Petersburg, FL 33705
Capacity: 45,360
Opening day: March 31, 1998—Detroit Tigers 11, Tampa Bay Devil Rays 6
Cost to construct: $138 million
Architect: HOK Sport; Lescher & Mahoney Sports
Dimensions (ft):
Left Field—315
Left Center—370
Center Field—404
Right Center—370
Right Field—322
Defining feature: Left Field "Beach"
Little-known ground rule: A batted ball that hits either of the lower two catwalks, lights, or suspended objects in fair territory is a home run
Most expensive seat: $80
Cheapest seat: $6
World Series: none
All-Star Game: none

Memorable moments:
1999 May 2—Jose Canseco hits a towering blast onto a catwalk. When the ball doesn't come down, he is awarded a double.
1999 August 7—Wade Boggs gets his 3,000th hit, a home run.
2000 September 17—Devil Rays game with the Oakland Athletics is postponed because of Hurricane Gordon, only the third domed game ever postponed by weather.

If you build it, they will come.

That was the hope of stadium investors and Florida baseball fans when the Florida Suncoast Dome (as it was then known) was completed in 1986. The state-of-the-art stadium had everything a modern park needed except a team. Business leaders tried to lure the White Sox, the Twins, and the Expos, but failed. A local businessman even purchased the San Francisco Giants for $113 million, but the move was rejected by major league owners. ("No team should be able to move nilly-willy," said Texas Ranger managing partner George W. Bush at the time.)

Major League Baseball finally rewarded Florida's baseball-starved fans the expansion Devil Rays in 1996, after owners agreed to spend $85 million to convert what had become known as the Thunderdome, home of the NHL Lightnings, into a baseball haven.

Purists frown on domed stadiums. Nevertheless, Tropicana Field, as it was named when it reopened, was made exclusively for baseball. Inspired by Ebbets Field, a grand, eight-story high rotunda greets fans as they enter.

The asymmetrical outfield dimensions closely match those from the old Brooklyn Dodger home. Seats are just 50 feet behind home plate, among the closest in the majors. To mimic the look of an outdoor stadium, the field features all-dirt base paths on artificial turf, the first major-league park to do so since St. Louis' Busch Stadium two decades earlier. The natural look is enhanced by FieldTurf, a new and realistic-looking form of synthetic grass that combines artificial grass with sand and ground rubber.

Dubbed "the Ballpark of the 21st Century" by team owner Vince Naimoli the year it opened, the stadium is loaded with amenities. The main rotunda features 1.8 million color tiles and a sound system delivering play-by-play of memorable baseball moments. The Center Field Street includes a cigar bar and restaurant, a billiards hall, a brew house, and a climbing wall. A restaurant in the batter's line of vision in dead center field is aptly named the "Batter's Eye." An area known as "The Beach" in left field's second deck features palm trees, a spa, a restaurant, and ushers dressed in Hawaiian shirts. A Devil Rays' home victory is announced to the outside by lighting the roof of Tropicana Field orange.

Tropicana Field has the world's second-largest cable-supported domed roof (after the Georgia Dome in Atlanta). The Teflon-coated fiberglass slants at a distinct angle. With hurricanes in mind, the roof is built to withstand wind up to 115 miles per hour. Among the most versatile parks, the stadium has hosted 16 other sports, including basketball, football, sprint car and motorcycle racing, gymnastics, soccer, tennis, weight-lifting, karate, motorcycle racing, equestrian events, track, figure skating, and ping pong.

Right: Inside the dome of Tropicana Field, home of the Tampa Bay Devil Rays since 1998.
Digitalballparks.com

Far left: Palm trees flank the entrance to Tropicana Field.
Digitalballparks.com

Left: Tropicana left field from upper deck.
Digitalballparks.com

TORONTO BLUE JAYS

SKYDOME

TORONTO BLUE JAYS

Address:
One Blue Jays Way Suite 3200
Toronto, Ontario M5V 1J1
Capacity: 50,516
Opening day: June 5, 1989—Milwaukee Brewers 5,
Toronto Blue Jays 3
Cost to construct: $500 million
Architect: Rod Robbie and Michael Allen
Dimensions (ft):
Left Field—328
Left Center—375
Center Field—400
Right Center—375
Right Field—328
Defining feature: Retractable dome
Little-known ground rule: The decision as to
whether a game begins with the roof open or closed
rests solely with the Toronto Blue Jays. If the game
begins with the roof closed: It shall not be opened at
any time during the game
World Series: 1992, 1993
All-Star Game: 1991

Memorable moments:
1989 August 4—Blue Jay Pitcher David Stieb loses a no-
hitter against the Yankees with two outs in the
ninth inning on a Roberto Kelly double.
1989 October 7—Oakland's Jose Canseco hits a 500-
plus foot home run into the fifth deck during
game four of the league championship series.
1992 September 4—Blue Jays hit 10 consecutive hits
against the Minnesota Twins, tying an AL record.
1993 October 23—Joe Carter's ninth-inning, three-run
homer to the left field seats wins the World
Series over Philly 8–6 for Toronto's second consecutive world championship.
1998 July 5—Roger Clemens records his 3,000th
career strikeout.

Baseball has always been afraid of the elements, suffering through cold springs and canceling games in the rain. And then came SkyDome.

With its retractable roof, the first for any sports arena in the world, engineers figured out how to make baseball playable from April though October, even in the frigid north. Balancing 22 million tons 31 stories in the sky, SkyDome takes 20 minutes to open or close its four rooftop panels, which cover 340,000 square feet.

When it is open, downtown's trademark CN Tower looms over right field, and the downdraft makes home runs difficult. When it is closed, the dome is among the tallest in the majors, and the park turns into a hitter's field.

The perfectly symmetrical SkyDome was state-of-the-art when it opened, just six years before quirky Camden Yards would touch off a revival of uniquely shaped ballparks. The pitchers' mound is constructed on a fiberglass dish which allows it to be raised or lowered by hydraulics, and eight miles of zippers connect the strips of artificial turf .

Home to the Canadian Football League's Toronto Argonauts, SkyDome is more than just baseball. The building contains a 348-room Renaissance Hotel, with 70 rooms overlooking the playing field (where guests have exposed themselves in compromising positions more than once), a Hard Rock Cafe, a 300-foot bar with all seats facing the field, a health club with squash courts, a mini-golf course, and an indoor running track.

As much an architectural attraction as a sports venue, SkyDome was the first major-league park to exceed four million patrons in a single season, a feat it accomplished three years in a row. The stadium's $17 million, 33-foot by 110-foot Jumbotron video scoreboard with its 67,200 light bulbs is North America's largest.

The name SkyDome (not *the* SkyDome) was the product of a contest, selected from among 12,879 entries. The winner, Kellie Watson, was asked by the *Toronto Globe and Mail* to explain the name.

"It was dome," she responded, "where you could see the sky."

Right: External view of Toronto's SkyDome and the looming height of the CN Tower taken during the 1989 season.
Photo by Rick Stewart/Allsport via Getty Images

Right and Below: Two details of SkyDome. Note the base of the CN tower visible in the photo below. With the roof open, the downdraft from the tower makes batting a much more difficult job than when it's open.
Digitalballparks.com

Above and Above Right:
Game 2 of the 1993 World Series between the Blue Jays and the Philadelphia Phillies.
Photo by Rick Stewart/Allsport via Getty Images

Left: Inside SkyDome with the roof open; photo taken in 1989 from above home plate. *Photo by Rick Stewart/Allsport via Getty Images*

Left: Toronto's CN Tower rises over the SkyDome—creating real problems for sluggers.
Nik Wheeler/CORBIS

They are the best of parks. They are the worst of parks. The ball fields of the American League Central Division include Cleveland's Jacobs Field, so lovely it sold out 455 consecutive games, and Minnesota's Hubert H. Humphrey Metrodome, a baseball design so hideous that even Twins fans have demanded its demolition.

The American League central division includes one park from the 70s, one from the 80s, two from the 90s, and one from 2000. Though each offers its unique charms, Jacobs Field, Detroit's Comerica Park, and Kansas City's Kauffman Stadium, are all regarded as wonderful places to watch a baseball game. Chicago's U.S. Cellular Field—opened just a year before Baltimore's Camden Yards would incite a demand for old-fashioned retro-parks—is functional. And Minnesota's Hubert H. Humphrey Metrodome, with its dim lighting, its hefty bag outfield, and its bright, ball-losing, Teflon ceiling is barely that. The Twins have already drawn up plans for a new retractable dome stadium, though they are lacking the means to pay for it. The rest of the parks of the American League Central Division should be around for a while.

U.S. Cellular Field from home plate upper level during the game between the Cleveland Indians and the White Sox on June 21, 2003. The White Sox won 4-3.

Photo by Jerry Driendl/Getty Images

CHICAGO WHITE SOX

U.S. CELLULAR FIELD

CHICAGO WHITE SOX

Aka: Comiskey Park 1991–2002
Address:
333 West 35th St.
Chicago, Ill 60616
Capacity: 45,936
Opening day: April 18, 1991—Detroit Tigers 16, Chicago White Sox 0
Cost to construct: $167 million
Architect: HOK Sport
Dimensions (ft):
Left Field—330
Left Center—377
Center Field—400
Right Center—372
Right Field—335
Defining feature: Exploding scoreboard
Little-known ground rule: Any fair, batted ball that travels over the yellow line painted on the outfield fence is a home run
Most expensive seat: $40
Cheapest seat: $14
World Series: None
All-Star Game: 2003

Memorable moments:
1993 April 9—Bo Jackson homers on his first major-league swing.
1993 June 22—Carlton Fisk catches his 2,226th game, a major-league record.
1997 June 16—The Cubs beat the White Sox 8–3 in Chicago's first regular season hometown matchup. The Sox come back to win the next two.
1998 July 31—Albert Belle establishes a major-league record by hitting his 16th home run of the month.
2002 September 19—Father and son spectators run onto field and attack Royals first base coach Tom Gamboa.

The White Sox home was built under duress. Team owner Jerry Reinsdorf had issued the city an ultimatum: build a new ballpark or he'd take the team to Florida. The Illinois legislature resisted, but eventually agreed to build a park directly across the street from 80-year-old Comiskey Park, which Shoeless Joe Jackson and Luke Appling once called home and where Bill Veeck introduced the world to an exploding scoreboard and disco demolition night.

The new stadium saved baseball for Chicago's South Side. It also produced one of the most maligned ballparks of the modern era. Completed just one year before Camden Yards brought baseball back to the future, the park does not include many of the touches that have rendered new ballparks instant classics.

There is little inside to let you know that you are in one of America's great baseball cities. The field is almost exactly symmetrical. The top deck is far from the field, and rises at a harrowingly steep slope in order to expose the lower deck to the sky and make room for two tiers of money-making luxury boxes. How distant is the top deck? The front row of upper deck seats is further from the playing field than the back row at the Old Comiskey. Heavy winds off Lake Michigan have closed the upper deck on a few occasions for the safety of the fans.

Still, it was the first park built exclusively for baseball since Kansas City's Kauffman Stadium in 1973. Unlike its predecessor, there are wide concourses, lots of amenities, and no obstructed-view seats. The owners built a new exploding scoreboard, with pinwheels and fireworks set off by a White Sox home run. The retired uniforms of eight players are displayed at the park: Luke Appling (4), Nellie Fox (2), Minnie Minoso (9), Luis Aparicio (11), Ted Lyons (16), Billy Pierce (19), Carlton Fisk (72), and Harold Baines (3).

In its initial year, the reviews were not so bad, and 2,934,154 fans shattered the club's attendance record. It wasn't until Camden Yards opened the following year that fans began to realize what they had missed out on in Chicago.

The White Sox sold the naming rights to U.S. Cellular for 20 years at a price of $68 million in 2003, depriving baseball of one of its best known names (for all of his playing, managing, and owning days, what Charlie Comiskey is best remembered for is his stinginess toward his players that contributed to the "Black Sox" scandal of 1919.) The club has pledged to spend generously on stadium renovations. The fences have been moved in, a huge high-resolution video screen has been installed in the scoreboard, and a new fan deck, which allows fans to peer over the outfield from above the batter's line of vision in center field, has been added.

Just like old Comiskey, U.S. Cellular Field is a looming fixture on the Dan Ryan Expressway. For nearly two years, the two stadiums stood side-by-side, monuments to the past and the future, before wrecking balls did away with the past.

Left: For 80 years, until 1990, the home of the Chicago White Sox, Comiskey Park was also home to so many baseball greats, among them Shoeless Joe Jackson, Luke Appling, Nellie Fox, Minnie Minoso, and Luis Aparicio. The era of Bill Veeck's ownership, which began in 1959, saw such innovations as the "exploding" scoreboard, player names on the back of team jerseys, and special promotional events such as the disastrous Disco Demolition Night.
National Baseball Hall of Fame

59

U.S. Cellular Field from press box level during
the All-Star Game between the Indians and the
White Sox on June 22, 2003.
Photo by Jerry Driendl/Getty Images

Right: Exterior of U.S. Cellular Field on June 22, 2003.
Photo by Jerry Driendl/Getty Images

COMISKEY PARK
(1910–90)

Home of the Chicago White Sox.

Comiskey Park opened just a few years before today's surviving gems: Wrigley Field, Fenway Park, and Yankee Stadium. Comiskey was a much larger park, built to create long runs for outfielders and thrilling extra-base hits, rather than uncontested home runs. Pitchers loved it. The park was home to baseball's first All-Star game in 1933.

In 1960, Bill Veeck rigged the scoreboard to explode after every White Sox home run, a Comiskey tradition that continues today. Another promotion in 1979 didn't work out so well. Veeck invited fans to Disco Demolition Night, charging just 98 cents for bleacher fans who brought disco records to burn between doubleheader games. The outfield inferno resulted in 50 arrests, and White Sox were forced to forfeit the second game.

Above: Five-year-old Brian Jones sings the national anthem with his proud father, DeNard Jones, kneeling beside him.
Time Life Pictures/Getty Images

Right: A view from the press box at Comiskey Park during the 1959 World Series.
Time Life Pictures/Getty Images

Far Right: The new owner of the Chicago White Sox, Bill Veeck, standing in a snowy Comiskey Park.
Time Life Pictures/Getty Images

Far Left: July 23, 1995—a view of Comiskey Park taken during a game between the White Sox and the Milwaukee Brewers. *Photo by Jonathan Daniel/Allsport via Getty Images*

Left: Spectator joy as the White Sox defeat the Red Sox 1-0 in the tenth inning, at Old Comiskey Park. *Time Life Pictures/Getty Images*

CLEVELAND INDIANS

JACOBS FIELD

CLEVELAND INDIANS: JACOBS FIELD

Address:
2401 Ontario Street
Cleveland, OH 44115
Capacity: 43,368
Opening day: April 4, 1994—Cleveland Indians 4, Kansas City 3 (11 innings)
Cost to construct: $175 million
Architect: HOK Sports
Dimensions (ft):
Left Field—325
Left Center—370
Center Field—405
Right Center—375
Right Field—325
Defining feature: Left field scoreboard
Little-known ground rule: Thrown ball that enters camera pits, dugouts, or diamond suites and remains: two bases
Most expensive seat: $50
Cheapest seat: $5
World Series: 1995, 1997
All-Star Game: 1997

Memorable moments:
1994 April 4—Wayne Kirby's 11th-inning single gives Cleveland a 4-3 victory in the Jake's debut.
1995 September 8—Cleveland defeats Baltimore 3–2 to clinch the AL Central Division, its first championship in 41 years.
1995 September 30—Albert belle hits 50th home run, most in Indians' history, until Jim Thome cracks 52 seven years later.
1997 July 8—Hometown catcher Sandy Alomar hits a seventh-inning, two-run homer to lead the AL to a 3–1 All-Star game victory.
2001 August 5—Trailing the Mariners 14–2, the Tribe scores 13 unanswered runs for their greatest comeback in 76 years.

They serve pirogues and sushi at the Jake.

After playing for 61 years at cavernous Municipal Stadium at the edge of Lake Erie, derisively labeled the "mistake by the lake," the Indians moved into a boutique park where the blend of old and new is among the wonders of modern baseball.

Where the old stadium looked like something a child would build with an advanced erecter set, Jacobs Field was carefully sculpted to blend Indians' baseball with Cleveland's industrial roots.

The architects boast of using the city's traditional stone and brick masonry and providing direct views into the park from two street-level plazas to further integrate it with the city. Critics have credited the lattice work on the exterior for reflecting the bridges that cross the Cuyahoga River and the light standards for mimicking the industrial city's smokestacks. The result is an urban structure that is an integral part of Cleveland's downtown renaissance.

While the old stadium offered little more than a baseball diamond and seats, the Jake is a feast for the eyes. An appealing panorama of downtown Cleveland, if such a thing is possible, rises over the outfield, as does a 120-foot tall, 222-foot wide scoreboard, the largest freestanding scoreboard in the majors. The left-field scoreboard is reachable only by the likes of Mark McGwire, who did it off Orel Hershiser on April 30, 1997. Seats are angled to face the action at the plate.

Some elements resemble other parks. The 19-foot tall left-field fence, is referred to as the "mini-green monster." The bleachers compare to Wrigley's. Like most old parks, the playing field is anything but symmetric. Dead center field is not as deep as deepest left center. There is a triple deck in right. Home plate was transplanted from the old Municipal Stadium.

The new park is named after Richard Jacobs, who bought the Indians in 1985 and paid for the stadium's naming rights. The new home has suited the Indians well. Perennial losers, the Tribe won five consecutive division titles from 1995 to 1999. The stadium was sold out for a record 455 consecutive games, which would have been unimaginable at its old home.

Right: Players line the baselines as a brass band prepares to play the national anthem before a game between the Kansas City Royals and the Cleveland Indians. The Indians won 11–2. *Photo by Tom Pidgeon/Getty Images*

Following page, Left: Bernie Williams—#51 of the New York Yankees—leaps up to catch a home run hit and misses the ball during the game against the Indians at Jacobs Field on May 26, 2001. The Yankees defeated the Indians 12–5. *Photo by Tom Pigeon /Allsport via Getty Images*

Following page, Right: General view of the stadium during the opening day game at Jacobs Field April 8, 2002. The Indians won 9–5. *Photo by Tom Pidgeon/Getty Images*

Right: Officially christened Lakefront Stadium when it opened 1932, but more popularly known among fans of the resident Cleveland Indians as the "Mistake by the Lake," Municipal Stadium was used by the Indians until 1993
National Baseball Hall of Fame

Far Right: After the last baseball game played in Cleveland Municipal Stadium in October of 1993, it continued in service as the home of the NFL Browns, until it was demolished in 1996 following the Browns departure for Baltimore. Now a new "Cleveland Browns" team plays in Cleveland Browns Stadium built in 1997 on the site of the original Municipal Stadium while the Cleveland Indians have played some of the best baseball in their long history at the critically acclaimed Jacobs Field since 1994.
National Baseball Hall of Fame

DETROIT TIGERS

COMERICA PARK

DETROIT TIGERS

Address:
2100 Woodward Ave.
Detroit, MI 48201
Capacity: 40,120
Opening day: April 11, 2000—Detroit Tigers 5, Seattle Mariners 2
Cost to construct: $300 million
Architect: HOK Sports
Dimensions (ft):
Left Field—346
Left Center—402
Center Field—422
Right Center—379
Right Field—330
Defining feature: Scoreboard tigers
Little-known ground rule: Ball passing through or under the bullpen fence: two bases
Most expensive seat: $60
Cheapest seat: $5
World Series: None
All-Star Game: 2005 (scheduled)

Memorable moments:
2000 April 11—Fans endure 34-degree temperatures to watch the Tigers beat Seattle in the park's first game.
2000 August 23—Swarms of flying ants send fans fleeing.
2000 October 1—Shane Halter plays all nine positions on the final game of the season, the fourth major leaguer to do so.

It is ironic that Detroit's baseball team moved from a place called Tiger Stadium. It is at Comerica Park that tigers roam.

Large tiger statues greet visitors outside. The perimeter is lined with tigers holding baseballs (actually lights) in their mouths. Two enormous tigers are positioned at either side of the scoreboard, who roar when the home team hits a home run. A merry-go-round featuring 30 hand-painted tigers entertains children along the first base side. There are even tiger claw marks scratched into concrete pillars around the park.

Comerica Park is a far cry from the no-nonsense, old-fashioned ambiance of Tiger Stadium which sat on the well-worn intersection of Michigan and Trumbull, a corner where baseball was played for more than a century. Comerica Park's Ferris wheel (carriages are shaped like baseballs), its multi-colored water fountain that shoots "liquid fireworks," the air-conditioned bar, enormous state-of-the-art scoreboard, and the lack of a single pillar to block the view, would have been unthinkable at Tiger Stadium.

Yet Comerica Park works to celebrate the city's rich baseball history.

Oversized sculptures cast in stainless steel along the center field wall show six Tiger greats in classic poses: Ty Cobb sliding spikes up, Willie Horton swinging, Al Kaline making a one-arm grab, along with Charlie Gehringer, Hank Greenberg and Hal Newhouser. Kaline's glove is positioned so that some day, some shot to deep center might just get caught.

The park's brick and steel construction and asymmetric dimensions mimic old parks, as does the dirt patch from the pitchers mound to home plate, a staple of turn-of-the-century fields. Originally the center-field flagpole was in play, just like at Tiger Stadium, though the fences were moved in and the flagpole now sits beyond the fence.

The park also frames a spectacular view of downtown Detroit, which has worked hard to keep baseball in the city.

Right: Comerica Park Entrance with Comerica Park Tigers by Michael Keropian.
Photo by: Richard Cummins/CORBIS

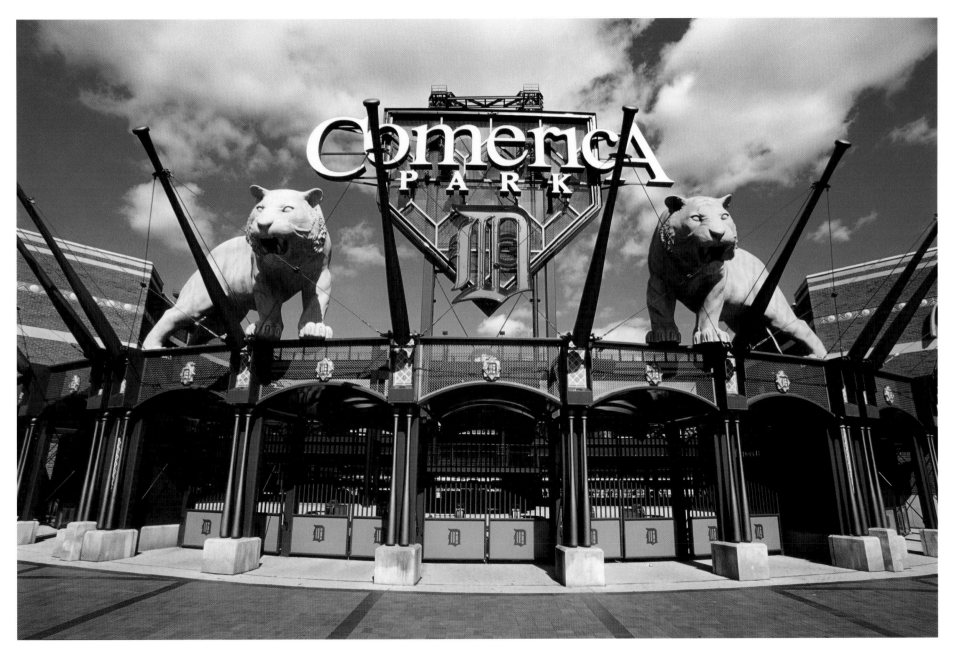

This page and Right: Two more views of Comerica Park.
National Baseball Hall of Fame (left); Mark Hertzberg/ National Baseball Hall of Fame (right)

TIGER STADIUM (1912–99)

Home of the Detroit Tigers

Tiger Stadium smelled like old-time baseball. The game was first played at the corner of Michigan and Trumbull, a healthy stroll from downtown, in 1896. Tiger Stadium, originally Navin Field, was opened in 1912, the same week the *Titanic* sank, and the same day that Fenway Park opened in Boston. By 1938, the stadium had been fully enclosed, able to capture the fragrance of hot dogs, peanuts, and Cracker Jack for thousands of games to come. The second deck provided some of the best seats in baseball, and produced dramatic home runs that would disappear into the upper stands. A 125-foot high, center field flagpole sat in fair territory along the center field fence until the 1930s.

Tiger Stadium remained a fixture through the careers of Ty Cobb, Charlie Gehringer, Hank Greenberg, Al Kaline, and Willie Horton. It was here, on May 2, 1939, that the Yankees Lou Gehrig asked to be removed from the lineup, ending his iron man streak at 2,130 games.

With its obstructed views and rusted pillars, Tiger Stadium was in need of major repair by the 1990s, when the Tigers considered enclosing it with a dome and finally decided that a new facility was needed. Today the stadium remains standing as city planners try to figure out what else belongs at the famed Detroit corner.

Right: c. 1937 aerial view of Tiger Stadium. The upper deck was constructed over the outfield bleachers in this year; and the 125-foot flag-pole in center field was removed at the end of the season.
National Baseball Hall of Fame

The Final Game
Michigan & Trumbull
Sept. 27, 1999
Detroit vs. Kansas City

Left: Tiger Stadium taken on the occasion of the last game—Kansas City versus Detroit on September 27, 1999.
National Baseball Hall of Fame

KANSAS CITY ROYALS

KAUFFMAN STADIUM

KANSAS CITY ROYALS

Aka: Royals Stadium 1973–93
Address:
1 Royal Way
Kansas City, MO 64141
Capacity: 40,793
Opening day: April 10, 1973—Kansas City Royals 12, Texas Rangers 1
Cost to construct: $70 million
Architect: HNTB and Charles Deaton Design Associates
Dimensions (ft):
Left Field—330
Left Center—375
Center Field—400
Right Center—375
Right Field—330
Defining feature: Outfield waterworks
Most expensive seat: $25
Cheapest seat: $8
World Series: 1980, 1985

Memorable moments:
1973 May 15—Nolan Ryan of the California Angels strikes out 12 Royals in his first of seven career no-hitters.
1976 October 3—George Brett hits an inside-the-park home run on a misplayed ball to edge teammate Hal McRae for the AL batting title in the season's final at-bat.
1977 May 14—Jim Colborn pitches Royal's first no-hitter at the stadium, beating Texas 6–0.
1980 August 17—George Brett's goes four-for-four and raises his batting average to .400
1985 October 27—Royals win their first World Series on Bret Saberhagen's game seven shutout over St. Louis.
1985 October 26—First base umpire Don Denkinger's blown call on a Jorge Orta ground ball in the bottom of the ninth inning of game six gives the Royals a chance to tie the World Series. The Royals go on to beat their cross state rivals, the St. Louis Cardinals, 11–0 the following day.
1986 September 14—Bo Jackson hits his first major-league home run, a 475-foot blast believed to be the longest in stadium history.
1991 August 26—Bret Saberhagen no-hits the White Sox.

If baseball stadiums are urban cathedrals, then Kauffman stadium is a rogue church.

There is no Waveland Avenue or Lansdowne Street hugging the fence at Kauffman Stadium, just freeway and farmland. Approaching from the West, one could drive hundreds of miles without seeing lights as bright as the standards atop the stadium, which draw insects from acres around.

Yet it is orthodox baseball they worship inside, as devout as anywhere else. At a time when other cities were building multi-sports complexes, the Royals was the only franchise to build a baseball-only stadium during the 60s, 70s, and 80s. The site lines and seats all point toward the action. Grass replaced artificial turf in 1995, the fences were moved in, and the walls lowered.

Known for most of its life as Royals Stadium, it was renamed in honor of Ewing M. Kauffman who purchased the expansion team for Kansas City in 1968. If you want to date a color photo of Kauffman Stadium look at the seats. By the end of 2000, all of the red seats had been replaced by new blue ones. Intentionally located at the junction of I-70 and I-435, passersby can catch glimpses inside the park as they drive by.

If there is any monument to the era in which it was built, it is the 12-story high scoreboard, containing 16,320 lights, with a huge Royals crown on top, a Midwest version of Anaheim's Big A. The park's signature feature is a 322-foot wide water fountain spectacular—the largest privately funded waterworks in the world—which occupies the space that bleachers normally would, offering water-filled entertainment between innings.

Right: View of a game between the Toronto Blue Jays and the Royals at Kauffman Stadium on June 11, 1995. The Royals won the game 2–1.
Photo by Stephen Dunn/Allsport via Getty Images

Above: Night game at Royals Stadium.
National Baseball Hall of Fame

Far Left: General view of action during a game between the Red Sox and the Royals at Royals Stadium.
Getty Images

Left: The Truman Sports Complex comprises the Royals Stadium (lower) and Arrowhead Stadium, home of the NFL Kansas City Chiefs.
National Baseball Hall of Fame

MINNESOTA TWINS

HUBERT H. HUMPHREY METRODOME

MINNESOTA TWINS:
HUBERT H. HUMPHREY METRODOME

Address:
34 Kirby Puckett Place
Minneapolis, MN 55415
Capacity: 48,678
Opening day: April 6, 1982—Seattle Mariners 11, Minnesota Twins 7
Cost to construct: $68 million
Architect: Skidmore, Owings & Merrill
Dimensions (ft):
Left Field—343
Left Center—385
Center Field—408
Right Center—367
Right Field—327
Defining feature: High decibel postseason noise
Little-known ground rule: Ball hitting roof or speakers in fair territory: if caught by fielder, batter is out and runners advance at their own risk
Most expensive seat: $35
Cheapest seat: $6
World Series: 1987, 1991
All-Star Game: 1985

Memorable moments:
1984 May 4—Oakland's Dave Kingman hits a towering shot into one of the roof's drainage holes. The ball never comes down and Kingman, is awarded a ground-rule double.
1987 October 7—Gary Gaetti hits two home runs to lead Twins over Tigers in the team's first postseason game in 17 years.
1991 October 26—Kirby Puckett goes three-for-four, makes an astounding center-field catch, and hits an 11th-inning home run to force a seventh World Series game vs. Atlanta.
1991 October 27—Jack Morris pitches 10 shutout innings as Twins win the seventh game of the World Series over Atlanta 1-0.
1993 September 16—Dave Winfield collects his 3,000th hit.

Few stadiums in baseball are more maligned than downtown Minneapolis' dome. The Metrodome is loud, indoors, poorly carpeted, a hard place to spot balls, and a far, far cry from a field of dreams—unless you are a Twins fan.

It is here that the underrated Twins won the World Series in 1987 and 1991 without winning a single game in a National League park. It is here that Kirby Puckett and Torii Hunter turned a flexible baggy-like wall into a tool of defensive beauty. It is here that the descendents of Harmon Killebrew and Tony Oliva can play baseball for six (and sometimes seven) months a year in a climate better suited for hockey.

Few fields are more loaded with home-field advantages. The white Teflon roof makes it difficult to pick up high-fly balls, particularly during day games. The screams of the homer hanky-waving fans in the 1987 World Series were measured by *Sporting News* at 118 decibels, about the same as a jet airplane on take-off. The odd curvature behind home plates makes wild pitches routinely rebound toward first base.

The Twins have used it to their advantage. In their first World Championship season in 1987, the Twins were 56–25 in the Metrodome during the regular season, and 29–52 on the road. They went on to win the World Series by winning every game at home, a feat they would repeat four years later, prompting many opposing fans to call for the dome's destruction. Higher walls and fixes to the air-conditioning system have stripped the park of its reputation as a "homer dome," and a new artificial turf makes the ball bounce less. Yet the park is still regarded as among the worst venues in baseball.

The Hubert H. Humphrey Metrodome, named after the former mayor, senator, and vice president, was built at a time when the economy of sports demanded that facilities house many activities. It is the only facility, as the Twins boast, to host the World Series (1987 and 1991), baseball's All-Star Game (1985), the Super Bowl (XXVI, 1992) and the NCAA Final Four basketball tournament (1992 and 2001), not to mention the Rolling Stones and Metallica, Billy Graham, several monster truck competitions, and hundreds of touch-football matches.

The Teflon-coated fiberglass ceiling rises almost 20 stories in the air, and it is the only air-supported dome in the major leagues. Fans feel a whoosh of air as they enter the park through revolving doors that prevent the escape of air that keeps the dome afloat. Heavy snow has torn the dome on several occasions, once forcing the Twins to postpone an April game with the Angels. The roof has come into play on numerous occasions. In 1992, Chili Davis hit a towering drive which bounced off a speaker dangling from the roof, which rather than being a home run, ricocheted into the glove of Baltimore second baseman Mark McLemore for an out. The same year, Detroit's Rob Deer hit two balls off the roof in consecutive innings, both of which were caught by shortstop Greg Gagne.

Talk of a new stadium has been brewing in the Twin Cities for years. At the conclusion of the 2003 season, Minnesota Governor. Tim Pawlenty vowed: "The Twins and the Vikings are not going to remain in the Metrodome much longer."

External view of the Hubert
H. Humphrey Metrodome in
Minneapolis.
Getty Images

Left: Exterior view of the Metrodome.
Photo by: Joseph Sohm; ChromoSohm Inc./CORBIS

The Hubert H. Humphrey
Metrodome in Minneapolis.
Getty Images

METROPOLITAN STADIUM (1961–81)
Home of the Minnesota Twins

The Met was the ultimate suburban stadium, built on developing farmland, where parking was plentiful and far from bustling downtown. Its hodgepodge of grandstands and bleachers, surrounding a perfectly symmetrical field, was the result of a quick transformation from a minor league to a major league park, speeded up to lure the Twins from Washington. The grounds crew had a reputation for tailoring the infield to suit their team, which hosted a World Series in 1965, the team's fifth year in the Twin Cities. Minnesota's northern climate made outdoor games a challenge in April and September, let alone October, and by the early 1980s the Twins were playing downtown under a dome. The Mall of America now thrives on the site where the Met once stood.

GRIFFITH STADIUM
(1911–61)
Home of the Washington Senators

"First in war, first in peace, and last in the American League," was the standing joke about the Washington Senators who spent half a century toiling in a ballpark so large that in four separate seasons the team could muster just a single home run in their home park.

It was at Griffith Stadium, about two-and-a-half miles from the White House, where William Taft became the first president to throw out a ceremonial first pitch, a ritual that was repeated by presidents through John Fitzgerald Kennedy. The centerfield indent, which made room for five duplexes that could not be razed, along with a large tree beyond the fence, gave the park a distinct character. The left field foul line, which at one point was 405 feet from home plate, made it a friendly park for pitchers, like Hall of Famer Walter Johnson, who called it home. Though the Senators had only fleeting moments of glory, it was also home to the successful Homestead Grays of the Negro League, and to Josh Gibson, who may have been professional baseball's finest power hitter.

After the 1960 season, the team moved to Minnesota and became the Twins. A new Senators team began playing at Griffith Stadium the very next year, but a desire for a more modern home prompted a move to Capitol Hill's RFK stadium. Griffith Stadium was knocked down in 1965.

Left: Just two-and-a-half miles from the White House, Griffith Stadium was the home of the Washington Senators for fifty years.For the 1961 season, the team moved to Minnesota and became the Twins. A new Senators team played at Griffith for a short time before moving to the newly built RFK Stadium. One of the distinctive features of Griffith was a 30-foot high wall that extended most of the length of right field, similar to famous "Green Monster" at Boston's Fenway Park. Griffith was knocked down in 1965.
Martin Luther King, Jr. Library/National Baseball Hall of Fame

Right: American baseball player Stanley "Bucky" Harris (1896–1977), playing for the Washington Senators, lands on home plate after scoring a home run during the seventh game of the World Series at Griffith Stadium, Washington, D.C., October 10, 1924. Washington won the game and the series.
Getty Images

Inset Right: Clark Griffith stadium, opening day, April 1, 1957.
Time Life Pictures/Getty Images

AMERICAN LEAGUE WEST

The teams of the American League West are relatively young and so are their stadiums. The Athletics, who originally played in Philadelphia in the early 1900s, before moving to Kansas City in the 50s, and eventually to Oakland, are the only exception. The Anaheim Angels (originally the Los Angeles Angels, then the California Angels) came to life in the 60s, as did the Texas Rangers (from Washington), and the Seattle Mariners were born in 1977.

The Texas Rangers and the Seattle Mariners moved into new stadiums in the 1990s to rave reviews from their fans, who in the team's original homes had been subjected to Arlington's blistering heat and Seattle's impersonal dome. Anaheim has been quite comfortable in its home down the road from Disneyland since 1966. And Oakland A's fans enjoyed their over-sized coliseum until the NFL Raiders returned in 1998, turning a baseball friendly stadium into a football arena uncomfortably forced to hold 82 base-ball games a year.

The A's would like to build a park of their own, but after Seattle spent more than $500 million on its new park, it may be many years before Oakland follows suit.

Right: The exterior of the Ballpark in Arlington before a game between the Seattle Mariners and the Texas Rangers on July 6, 2003. The Rangers defeated the Mariners 5-1.
Photo by Ronald Martinez/Getty Images

ANAHEIM ANGELS

ANGEL STADIUM OF ANAHEIM

ANAHEIM ANGELS

Aka: Edison Field (1998–2003)
Anaheim Stadium (1966-1997)
Address:
Anaheim Stadium (1966–97)
2000 Gene Autry Way
Anaheim, CA 92806
Capacity: 45,050
Opening day: April 19, 1966—Chicago White Sox 3,
California Angels 1
Cost to construct: $24 million
Architect: Robert A.M. Stern, HOK (renovations)
Dimensions (ft):
Left Field—330
Left Center—365
Center Field—400
Right Center—365
Right Field—330
Defining feature: The Big A
Most expensive seat: $44
Cheapest seat: $9
World Series: 2002
All-Star Game: 1967

Memorable moments:
1970 October 1—Alex Johnson collects two hits to edge
　Carl Yazstremski in the chase for the AL batting crown.
1973 September 27—Nolan Ryan strikes out 16 Twins to
　establish a new record of 383 season strikeouts.
1984 September 17—Reggie Jackson hits his 500th home run,
　17 years to the day after hitting his first, and in the
　same park.
1985 August 4—Rod Carew hits his 3,000th career hit.
1986 June 18—Don Sutton wins his 300th game against Texas.
1986 October 12—Dave Henderson hits a two-out, two-run
　homer off Donnie Moore, to defeat the Angels who
　were within one strike of their first World Series
　appearance.
1990 September 14—Ken Griffey Jr. and Ken Griffey Sr.
　become first father-son pair to hit back-to-back home
　runs.
2002 October 27—Garret Anderson's bases loaded double in
　the third inning breaks a 1-1 tie and leads the Angels to
　a 4-1 win over the San Francisco Giants in game seven
　of the World Series.

Like much of Orange County, Angel Stadium was built on an old citrus grove, where oranges, alfalfa, and corn once grew. Anaheim in the 1960s was rapidly shedding its rural past. When Anaheim Stadium, as it was then known, opened in 1966, Disneyland had been open for just a decade, and nearby Los Angeles was spreading without restraint.

In that context, the preposterously enormous, 230-foot "A" reaching over the left-field wall to the sky, with a huge scoreboard and Standard Oil advertisement in the middle, and a golden halo on the top, fit right in. Roughly modeled on Dodger Stadium, the state-of-the-art National League park where the Angels had spent the previous four seasons, the team's new home provided an identity for the "California Angels," owned by singing cowboy Gene Autrey.

The park had a distinct Southern California charm, palm trees, wide open concourses, and immaculate concession stands, a far cry from the urban grit of eastern parks. The location was selected for its suburban ease, its ready freeway access and abundant parking.

The inside was made for baseball and nothing else. Short walls left outfielders to battle spectators for long fly balls. The triple deck contained no obstructed views. For its first two decades, the stadium had no bleachers at all, leaving the "Big A," and sometimes the distant San Gabriel mountains, looming as California icons.

The panoramic views ended after the 1979 season when the stadium was enclosed to add 20,000 seats for the NFL's Los Angeles Rams. The "Big A" was moved to the parking lot, where it remains today. In the 1990s, the Rams departed for St. Louis, the Disney Corp. assumed control of the Angels, and renovations were once again underway. This time $100 million was spent returning the park to its baseball-only status.

The 20,000 football seats were replaced with bleachers, a state-of-the-art scoreboard, and the "California spectacular," an improbable backdrop of geysers shooting water 90 feet in the air, waterfalls flowing down a rocky mountainside, artificial rocks, real trees, and the look of something straight out of Disneyland. Three full-service restaurants were added.

After nearly four decades of baseball in Anaheim, the Angels finally reached the World Series in 2002, which they won in dramatic style against the Giants in game seven, at home.

Right: A view of the baseball diamond taken during a game between the Detroit Tigers and the California Angels at Anaheim Stadium. The Angels defeated the Tigers 13–2. *Photo by Simon P. Barnett/Allsport via Getty Images*

Following page, Left: General view of Edison Field. *Photo by Jed Jacobsohn/Allsport via Getty Images*

Following page, Right: The Indians defeated the Angels 6–4 on April 5, 1998, in this game at the then Edison Field. Anaheim Stadium had become Edison International Field in 1996 under a $50 million, 20-year sponsorship deal. After five years, on December 30, 2003, the Anaheim Angels announced that they were going to rename their ballpark Angel Stadium of Anaheim for the 2004 season because Edison had decided to opt out of its naming rights agreement. *Photo by Jed Jacobsohn/Allsport via Getty Images*

OAKLAND A'S

NETWORK ASSOCIATES COLISEUM

OAKLAND A'S

Aka: Oakland-Alameda County Stadium 1968–97
Address:
UMAX Stadium, 1998
7000 Coliseum Way
Oakland, Ca. 94621
Capacity: 48,219
Opening day: April 17, 1968—Baltimore Orioles 4,
Oakland Athletics 1
Cost to construct: $25.5 million
Architect: Skidmore, Owings & Merrill
Dimensions (ft):
Left Field—330
Left Center—362
Center Field—400
Right Center—362
Right Field—330
Defining feature: Mount Davis
Most expensive seat: $34
Cheapest seat: $9
World Series: 1972, 1973 1974, 1988, 1989, 1990
All-Star Game: 1987

Memorable moments:
1968 May 8—Catfish Hunter pitches a perfect game
against the Minnesota Twins.
1972 September 22—Gene Tenace hits two RBI to lead
Oakland to a 3–2, World Series game seven victory over Cincinnati.
1979 April 17—Just 653 fans show up to watch the A's
beat the Mariners 6–5.
1988 October 18—Mark McGwire's ninth-inning home
run defeats Dodgers in World Series game three.
1991 May 1—Rickey Henderson steals third base for
his 939th stolen base, breaking Lou Brock's
record.

It is not with affection that A's fans refer to the dreary slab of luxury boxes, clubs, and sky high grandstands which killed the bleachers, the ice plants, and the view of the East Bay hills, as "Mount Davis." While the rest of the country was making their ballparks better, Oakland was going in the opposite direction.

The Oakland-Alameda County Stadium, as it was known until 1998, had always been a work-manlike like place to see a baseball game. Huge foul territories annoyed batters and kept fans too far from the action. The symmetry reflected the era in which it was built. It looked less like a ballpark than a coliseum.

But except for the distances, there wasn't a bad seat in the house. The plain concrete con-fines were accessible, the bleachers relaxing, and the view of the Oakland hills, scarred by a huge quarry in dead center, let you know that you were in one of baseball's finest climates.

And then Al Davis brought the Raiders back to Oakland.

The bleachers are now gone. The stadium is enclosed. And the new scoreboards are in perfect position only for a game with two end zones. The seats atop Mount Davis offer sweeping vistas of Mt. Tamalpais 20 miles in the distance, but no view of the warning track just below. Adding insult to the aesthetic change, the renovations weren't finished in time for the A's to begin their 1996 season, forcing them to open at a minor league park in Las Vegas. When fans were finally allowed back in (30 years to the day after then-Governor Ronald Reagan had thrown out the ceremonial first pitch at the stadium's inaugural game) they were given yellow construction hats with an A's logo.

The lack of collegiality between the football and baseball clubs is apparent on the A's Internet page, which refers dismissively to the coliseum as home to the Oakland Athletics and "Oakland's NFL franchise."

On the playing field, the wide foul territory is said to cost a batter five to seven batting average points over the course of a season, though it did not stop Reggie Jackson, Rickey Henderson, Jose Canseco, Mark McGwire, or Jason Giambi from hitting their stride. To the joy of most hitters, the fences have been moved in from their original locations, and the football enclosure keeps the wind down.

This was the home of Charlie Finley's innovations: orange baseballs, which were used in a 1973 exhibition game against the Indians, and gold-colored bases which adorned the infield for opening day 1970, a move the no-nonsense officials at Major League Baseball quickly banned. Besides the A's and Raiders, the coliseum was home to the USFL Oakland Invaders and has hosted scores of concerts from the Rolling Stones and the Who, to the Grateful Dead, Bruce Springsteen, and Bob Dylan.

Local lore has it that the coliseum was home to baseball's first "wave," on October 15, 1981, set off by the blond-haired, dugout-hopping, drum-pounding, wild man known as "crazy George," a development reviled by some base-ball fans almost as much as "Mount Davis."

Below: Fans sing "Take Me Out To The Ballgame" during the seventh-inning stretch at Oakland Coliseum 2000.
San Francisco Chronicle

Above: Oakland-Alameda County Stadium taken in May 1994. The stadium changed its name in 1998 to the Network Associates Coliseum.
National Baseball Hall of Fame

Left: The Coliseum before the start of a game between the Oakland Athletics and the Montreal Expos on June 15, 2003. The Athletics defeated the Expos 9-1.
Photo by: Justin Sullivan/Getty Images

Far Left: The Coliseum is dual-use with both football and baseball played. This shows the Coliseum during an NFL game between the Oakland Raiders and the Baltimore Ravens on December 14, 2003.
Getty Images

Left: The Seattle Mariners
play the Texas Rangers.
*Photo by: Paul A.
Souders/CORBIS*

Left: Exterior view of Safeco Field on June 25, 2003.
Getty Images

This page: Safeco Field with roof retracted. Built to the south of the Mariners' old home, the Kingdome (see next page), the new stadium was named after Safeco, a financial services company whose roots in Seattle date back to 1923. Safeco will pay $1.8 million per year for the next 20 years.
Photo by Otto Greule Jr/Getty Images

Left: When it opened in 1977, the Kingdome was the American League's first indoor stadium. In 1994 four ceiling tiles fell before the start of a game causing the team to play its final 15 games on the road. Repairs cost $70 million. The stadium, then home to the NFL Seahawks as well as the Mariners, was spectacularly demolished in 2000. A new football only stadium now occupies the site.
National Baseball Hall of Fame

Right: The dome itself was 660 feet in diameter and 250 feet from its apex to the playing surface. A batted ball hitting one of the speaker assemblies hung from the dome was considered to be in play. More than one hitter was "robbed" of a home run when a ball bouncing off a speaker was caught in flight for an out. Note the proximity to Puget Sound.
National Baseball Hall of Fame

TEXAS RANGERS

THE BALLPARK AT ARLINGTON

TEXAS RANGERS

Address:
1000 Ballpark Way
Arlington, TX 76011
Capacity: 49,292
Opening day: April 11, 1994—Milwaukee Brewers 4, Texas Rangers 3
Cost to construct: $191 million
Architect: HKS, Inc. and David M. Schwarz Architectural Services
Dimensions (ft):
Left Field—332
Left Center—390
Center Field—400
Right Center—381
Right Field—325
Defining feature: Center field office building
Little-known ground rule: Ball lodging in outfield fence padding or in the manually operated scoreboard in left field fence is a ground rule double
Most expensive seat: $75
Cheapest seat: $5
World Series: None
All-Star Game: 1995

Memorable moments:
1994 June 13—Jose Canseco hits three home runs and drives in eight runs in a 17–9 victory over Seattle.
1994 July 28—Kenny Rogers throws a perfect game against the Angels, the first Ranger to do so.
1996 April 19—Juan Gonzelez, Dean Palmer and Kevin Elster combine for 16 RBI as the Rangers beat O's 26–7
1996 September 15—Rangers retire Nolan Ryan's uniform, No. 34.
1997 June 12—In baseball's the first regular-season interleague game, San Francisco beats the Rangers 4–3.

Take a bit of Ebbets Field, some Tiger Stadium, a little Yankee Stadium, some Wrigley Field, and a touch of Camden Yards. Mix in a lot of Texas, put it in a suburban parking lot, and you approach the Ballpark at Arlington.

The asymmetrical outfield is like Ebbets Field, with eight facets sending hard-hit balls in different directions The double-decked, right-field porch is like Tiger Stadium, though it is too deep to catch as many home runs. The bleachers recall Wrigley. The canopy lining the upper deck is reminiscent of Yankee Stadium. The brick arches on the exterior feel like Camden Yards.

Yet this is Texas. Cast iron Lone Stars adorn aisles seats, replicating those on the building's facade. Large steer skulls and murals depicting the state's history decorate the walls, and a brick "Walk of Fame," celebrating Ranger's history surrounds the park. The grass in the batter's line of vision in dead center is named Greene's Hill after former Arlington Mayor Richard Greene. There is a Texas-sized dimension to the entire stadium complex, which includes a 12-acre, man-made lake (named for late Rangers broadcaster Mark Holtz), a 17,000 square-foot baseball museum said to be the largest outside Cooperstown, a 225-seat auditorium, a children's learning center, a four-story office building, and a kid-sized park with seats for 650 just outside.

To battle the Texas elements, the stadium is sunken, out of the wind, and enclosed by the office building, home to the Ranger's front office, just beyond center field. A giant wind-screen, 42 feet high and 430 feet long, was installed on the roof to further reduce wind. Overhead fans in the upper and lower deck porches help keep patrons cool.

The $191 million park was paid for largely through a sales tax increase, pushed through by the team's managing partner in the early 1990s, George W. Bush.

Right: Texas sized in every way, the Ballpark at Arlington contains a 12-acre man-made lake, a baseball museum said to be the largest after the Hall of Fame in Cooperstown, and a four-story office building.
National Baseball Hall of Fame

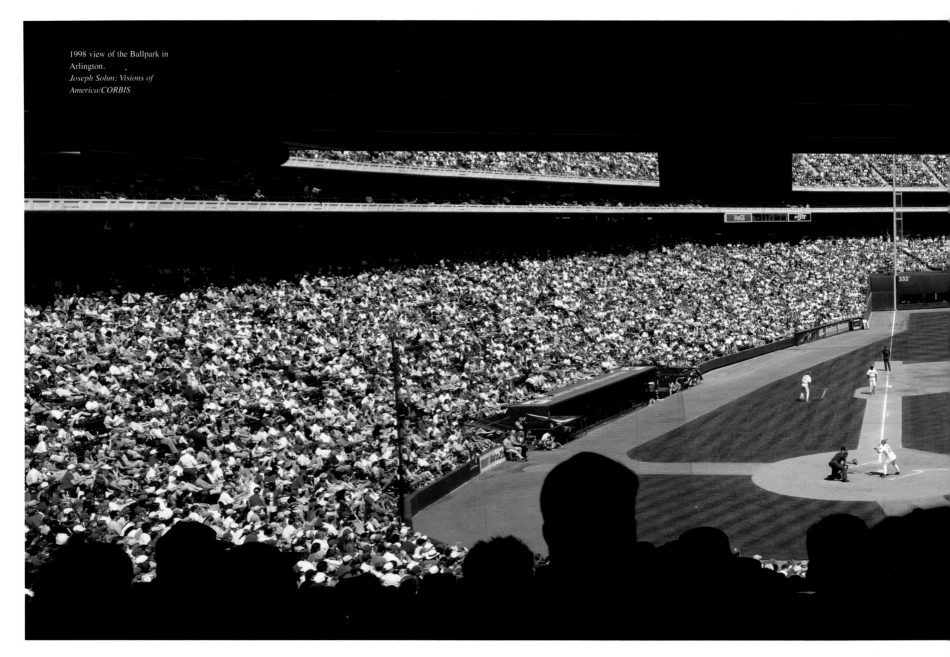

1998 view of the Ballpark in
Arlington.
*Joseph Sohm: Visions of
America/CORBIS*

Left: To provide the players some protection from the harsh Texas winds, the playing field is sunken and surrounded by tall, wind blocking structures and screens. *National Baseball Hall of Fame*

Far Left: A general view of the exterior of the Ballpark in Arlington before a game between the Seattle Mariners and the Texas Rangers on July 6, 2003. The Rangers defeated the Mariners 5–1. *Photo by Ronald Martinez/Getty Images*

Following page, Left: Another view of the Ballpark in Arlington on July 6, 2003. *Photo by Ronald Martinez/Getty Images*

Following page, Right: Heavy clouds loom over the ballpark during play between the Seattle Mariners and the Texas Rangers at the Ballpark in Arlington on July 6, 2003. *Photo by Ronald Martinez/Getty Images*

The National League of Professional Baseball Clubs, now known simply as the National League, was formed in 1876, the year of Custer's last stand, and exactly 100 years after the United States declared its independence. Some of its eight charter cities are familiar baseball towns: Chicago, Cincinnati, Philadelphia, St. Louis, and Boston. Others were unable to hold their teams: Hartford, Brooklyn, and Louisville.

The National League now consists of 16 teams, which have been divided into three divisions since 1994. Its newest franchises are located in places like Arizona and Colorado, which weren't even part of the union when the league was founded.

More than 80 National League parks have already opened and shut their doors. The old South End Grounds in Boston is now a T-station. The Hartford Ball Club Grounds now holds a church. Jefferson Grounds in Philadelphia, where on April 22, 1876, the first National League game was played, is now the site of an elementary school.

Today, the National League is experiencing a stadium explosion. Only five National League teams play in stadiums built prior to 1993. Seven new National League parks have been opened since 2000, including Citizen's Bank Park in Philadelphia and PETCO Park in San Diego, which opened their doors in 2004.

Left: Panorama of Turner Field as the Atlanta Braves play a night game in April 1997.
Joseph Sohm; ChromoSohm Inc./CORBIS

NATIONAL LEAGUE EAST

The National League East is a division of haves and have-nots. The pre-turn-of-the-century teams, the Braves and the Phillies, play in brand-new, highly regarded ball parks. The expansion clubs, the Mets, the Expos, and the Marlins, play in parks that most of their fans would just as soon abandon.

Two stadiums in the National League East Division were built for Olympics. Another was built for football. Montreal's Le Stade Olympique was constructed for the 1976 Summer Olympics, and converted for the Expos the following year. The result was an oversized, clumsy park that never felt quite right for base-ball. Twenty years later, the Braves learned from the Expos' mistakes. Atlanta's stadium for the 1996 Summer Games was specially designed to transform into a baseball friendly park.

Miami's Pro Player Stadium, the home of the NFL Dolphins and perfect for Sunday afternoons in the fall, was worked over to accommodate the Marlins' often overheated fans in the summer.

New York's Shea Stadium was built for base-ball, though it was also enlisted for football, con-certs, boxing matches, and religious events.

Philadelphia's Citizens, along with San Diego's Petco Park, are baseball's newest stadiums.

Fans in New York and Miami would like new stadiums. The Montreal Expos already play a quarter of their games in Puerto Rico as the team awaits a yet-to-be-determined new home.

Shea Stadium at dusk during the National League game between the Philadelphia Phillies and the New York Mets on July 13, 2003.
Photo by Jerry Driendl/Getty Images

ATLANTA BRAVES

TURNER FIELD

ATLANTA BRAVES

Address:
755 Hank Aaron Drive
Atlanta, GA 30315
Capacity: 49,304
Opening day: April 4, 1997—Atlanta Braves 5, Chicago Cubs 4
Cost to construct: $242.5 million
Architect: Atlanta Stadium Design Team
Dimensions (ft):
Left Field—335
Left Center—380
Center Field—401
Right Center—390
Right Field—330
Defining feature: 100 foot-high replica of Hank Aaron's 715 HR ball
Most expensive seat: $45
Cheapest seat: $1
World Series: 1999
All Star Game: 2000

Memorable moments:
1996 July 19—Muhammad Ali lights the Olympic flame atop the stadium that would become Turner Field.
1997 May 16—Michael Tucker breaks up a no-hitter by the Cardinals Alan Benes with two outs in bottom of ninth. Braves go on to win 1–0 in 13 innings.
1999 September 23—Chipper Jones hits his fourth home run in three games to complete a three-game sweep over division rival Mets.
1999 October 19—Andruw Jones draws an 11th-inning, bases-loaded walk to give the Braves a 10–9 victory over the Mets and their fifth National League pennant of the decade.

Turner Field was born an 85,000-seat, Olympic-sized track and field coliseum.

The Olympics came to Atlanta in 1996, just as the Braves were itching for a new home after playing for three decades in oversized Atlanta-Fulton County Stadium. In a confluence of creativity and good timing, the Braves and the city struck a deal.

The city built a $207 million Olympic stadium in the parking lot of the Braves' old home. Athletes from around the world paraded through the facility. Muhammad Ali lit the opening flame. When the Olympians went home, the Braves spent another $35 million to turn the mega-sports complex into a baseball-only facility.

The grandstands were ripped down and 35,000 seats were removed. Dugouts emerged from underneath Olympic bleachers. The Braves locker room was built in what was originally a basement TV studio.

The final product was a state-of-the-art, designer ballpark. It is more symmetric than the retro-parks now in fashion. But it offers intimate confines, seats angled toward home plate, and a brick and limestone facade reminiscent of Camden Yards.

Turner Field is not as old-fashioned looking as the other instant classics in Baltimore, Cleveland, or Pittsburgh, though it makes frequent gestures to Braves' history. Seats are decorated with a silhouette of Hank Aaron, whom many locals said the stadium should have been named after, rather than team owner Ted Turner.

It takes a close look to detect the stadium's Olympic lineage. One clue is the unusual outfield, where center and left field are curved, like stadiums built in the 1960s, a holdover from the oval-shaped Olympic Stadium, while the right field fence is a straight line consistent with today's old-style parks.

Outside the stadium, the tall posts that surround Monument Grove—a collection of statues which includes Hank Aaron, Warren Spahn, Eddie Matthews, Phil Niekro, Dale Murphy, and Georgia native Ty Cobb—are the very columns that supported the Olympic Stadium bleachers.

Off the field, the Brave's home resembles a theme park as much as a ballpark. Games, concessions (including food to reflect the visiting team, such as cheesesteaks when the Phillies are in town), and television monitors are ubiquitous. Near a Hall of Fame museum there is a video wall with televisions showing every major-league game in progress. The first fan who catches a home run in a far-away section in the third tier of left field has been promised $1 million, something that baseball experts and those who understand physics agree is unlikely to ever happen.

The Grand Entry Plaza features food and games, and is anchored by a 100-foot-in-diameter photograph of Hank Aaron's actual 715th home run ball. In 1997, the old stadium was imploded, and is now a parking lot for the new.

Right: 1999 view of Turner Field.
National Baseball Hall of Fame

Left: Turner Field in 1999. *National Baseball Hall of Fame*

Right: Javy Lopez—#8 of the Atlanta Braves—flies out to left fielder Miguel Cabrera of the Florida Marlins in the seventh inning of the game on July 23, 2003, at Turner Field. The Marlins defeated the Braves in 12 innings 5–4. *Photo by Jamie Squire/Getty Images*

Right: Kenny Lofton—#7 of the Chicago Cubs—bats against the Atlanta Braves in the second inning of the National League Divisional Series Game 2 on October 1, 2003 at Turner Field. The Braves defeated the Cubs 5–3.
Photo by Craig Jones/Getty Images

Far Right: Construction began in 1964 on a structure that needed to be open in time to receive the Milwaukee Braves who were scheduled to move to Atlanta in time to play on Opening Day 1966. Astonishingly, construction was completed a year early. After Hank Aaron hit his 500th home-run there on July 14, 1968, the park was sometimes referred to as the "House that Hank Built," a not so subtle reference to another ballpark made famous by the balls that George Herman Ruth hit out of it.
National Baseball Hall of Fame

ATLANTA-FULTON COUNTY STADIUM
(1966–96)
Home of the Atlanta Braves

The home of Braves was built in less than a year, which was part of what lured the team from its home in Milwaukee. Enclosed, symmetrical and modern, it was known as a place to hit home runs. The power of the park was enhanced by its elevation 1,000 feet above sea level, not as thin-aired as the mile high environs of Denver, but giving batters a few extra feet on long fly balls. The stadium's most famous home run came on opening day, April 8, 1974, when Hank Aaron hit No. 715 over the left field wall, sending him on a well photographed, round-the-bases trot into baseball immortality. The stadium served admirably for 30 years, hosting four World Series in the 1990s, as the once-woeful Braves became the team of the decade. The stadium's final game was a 1 to 0 loss to the New York Yankees in the 1996 World Series.

LORIDA MARLINS

O PLAYER STADIUM

FLORIDA MARLINS

Aka: Joe Robbie Stadium (1993–96)
Address:
2267 Dan Marino Blvd.
Miami, Florida 33056
Capacity: 42,531
Opening day: April 5, 1993—Florida Marlins 6,
Los Angeles Dodgers 3
Cost to construct: $115 million
Architect: HOK Sports
Dimensions (ft):
Left Field—330
Left Center—385
Center Field—434
Right Center—385
Right Field—345
Defining feature: Teal Monster
Little-known ground rule: If a ball strikes any
portion of the left-field scoreboard below the upper-
most edge, it is in play
World Series: 1997, 2003
All-Star Game: None

Memorable moments:
1996 May 11—Al Leiter throws a no-hitter to beat the
    Rockies 11–0.
1997 October 12—Livan Hernandez strikes out 15
    Braves in a 2–1 victory in game five of the NLCS.
1997 October 26—Edgar Renteria drives home the
    winning run in the bottom of the 11th inning to
    beat the Cleveland Indians in the seventh game of
    the World Series.
2000 May 8—Braves closer John Rocker drops the ball
    while standing on the mound in the bottom of the
    ninth inning, committing an unforgettable balk that
    gives the Marlins a 3–2 victory.
2003 October 22—Alex Gonzalez hits a line drive
    home run over the left field fence in the 12th
    inning to beat the NY Yankees in Game five of the
    World Series. The Marlins win the series in New
    York two days later.

The Florida Marlins' home was built for football. Its square dimensions and coliseum-like quality made it a perfect venue to watch the Miami Dolphins on fall weekends. So it took some doing, and about $10 million, to make it compatible for baseball, the first football stadium to be so converted.

A hydraulically operated pitchers mound was installed, a new press box for baseball media was added, and baseball locker rooms built. A long manual scoreboard, running for 200 feet between left and center fields, rises to a height of 33 feet and is known as the "Teal Monster."

Due to its football-sized dimensions, huge numbers of empty orange seats, trimmed in teal and blue, made for a colorful but empty appearance. The Marlins decided to close the upper deck with blue tarps, limiting capacity and lending the park a more intimate feel.

The field has its quirks. Balls bound off the Teal Monster. A clock atop the wall routinely robs batters of home runs. A notch in deep center field creates a funky area known as the "Bermuda Triangle," where it is possible to hit the ball 433 feet without leaving the park, a fine place to hit a triple.

The entrance to the park, surrounded by pastel colors and palm trees, is unmistakably Florida. So is the weather, which often makes it uncomfortably hot during day games and thunderstorming at night.

"Pick up the park and move it 500 miles north, and you've got a real winner," wrote ESPN columnist Jeff Merron.

The owners are already looking for ways to let the Marlins play under a retractable dome, either in downtown Miami, or perhaps even at Pro Player.

For such a young stadium in such a young baseball town, Pro Player has seen a remarkable amount of post-season excitement. In 1997, the Marlins stunned the baseball world by winning the World Series in seven games over the Cleveland Indians. Attendance suffered when the old owners sold off the team's best talent. But a new crop of Marlins repeated the triumph in 2003 with a surprise six-game World Series victory over the New York Yankees.

Left: For its first 10 years, Pro Player Stadium was known as Joe Robbie Stadium, home of the Miami Dolphins. When the expansion Florida Marlins chose Miami as their home, Joe Robbie was converted to a dual-use venue. Millions were spent on giving the park a makeover that would be suitable for a franchise that everyone in the area hoped would be as storied as that of its NFL tenant. Now after only six years of regular-season baseball, there are two World Series Championship flags flying at Pro Player. The Marlins have proven their right to share this beautiful park with the Dolphins.
Photofile/National Baseball Hall of Fame

Left and Below Two more views of Pro Player Stadium. Built by Wayne Huizenga after he had bought the Miami Dolphins, it cost $10 million to renovate it for baseball. In 1996 Pro Player, a division of Fruit-of-the-Loom, bought the naming rights to the stadium.
Digitalballparks.com

Right: An night exterior view of Pro Player Stadium.
Digitalballparks.com

Above: A view of the Olympic Stadium from the first base dugout. Montreal is a bilingual city. Baseball in Montreal reflects the dual linguistic practices of its host city. Games are preceded by the singing of the Canadian and American national anthems and all signs and announcements are presented in French and English. Even the ads on the billboards in Olympic Stadium are often a mix of the two languages.
Digitalballparks.com

Above and Left: Two views of the interior of the Olympic Stadium. A retractable dome was added in 1988, but it didn't work very well, often not at all, and was replaced in 1998 by a fixed roof. When in 1991 a chunk of concrete fell from the roof, the Expos had to play the last 13 home games on the road.
National Baseball Hall of Fame

Left, Inset: For the 2003 season, in an attempt to raise revenue, the Montreal Expos saw 22 of their home games moved to Puerto Rico. This detail shows the exterior of the San Juan Hiram Bithorn Stadium.
Digitalballparks.com

Left: Juan Hiram Bithorn Stadium left field. Named after the first major leaguer to hail from Puerto Rico, Hiram Bithorn broke into the big leagues with the Cubs in 1943.
Digitalballparks.com

NEW YORK METS

SHEA STADIUM

NEW YORK

Address:
126th Street and Roosevelt Ave.
Queens, NY 11368
Capacity: 55,601
Opening day: April 17, 1964—Pittsburgh Pirates 4, New York Mets 3
Cost to construct: $25.5 million
Architect: Praeger-Kavanagh-Waterbury
Dimensions (ft):
Left Field—338
Left Center—378
Center Field—410
Right Center—378
Right Field—338
Defining feature: Noisy jets flying in and out of La Guardia
Most expensive seat: $53
Cheapest seat: $8
World Series: 1969, 1973, 1986, 2000
All-Star Game: 1964

Memorable moments:
1964 June 21—Philadelphia's Jim Bunning pitches a perfect game against the Mets, striking out 10, and driving in two runs.
1965 August 15—The Beatles open a U.S. tour before 60,000 screaming fans.
1966 April 11—Tommy Agee becomes the first player to hit a ball into Shea's upper deck.
1968 April 19—Mets Nolan Ryan strikes out the Dodgers on nine consecutive pitches.
1969 October 15—Tom Seaver pitches the Mets to victory over the Orioles, as Ron Swoboda makes a run-saving catch in the ninth inning, and J.C. Martin bunts home a run in the 11th. The Mets win their first World Series the following day.
1986 October 25—Boston first baseman Bill Buckner lets a Mookie Wilson ground ball roll through his legs in the 11th inning, allowing Ray Knight to score the winning run in a come-from-behind victory. The Mets beat the Red Sox again the next day to win the World Series.
1996 May 11—An 18-minute, benches-clearing brawl on "John Franco Day," leads to nine ejections, including Franco's.
2000 October 16—Mike Hampton pitches a three-hit shutout over St. Louis as the Mets win their first pennant since 1986.

Few parks in baseball possess so many memories and so little soul.

Opened in an era of cookie-cutter parks, Shea's builders boasted of its symmetrical geometry, its grand four-story escalator system, its tall ramps, its tidy four-tier layout, and its lack of view-blocking pillars. It was the first stadium built able to make a rapid transition to football, and one of the first to feature a novel "color" scoreboard.

It was a wonder in a time gone by. Today, its most remarkable feature is its noise, which has nothing to do with its fans, but the stadium's unfortunate location in the flight path of New York La Guardia Airport, which averages more than 1,000 flights a day. The disrupting engine roar, which has prompted some players to wear earplugs, is a constant reminder that this is not a quaint ball yard.

Still, it was here that Tom Seaver and Nolan Ryan began their careers, and Willie Mays finished his. It is here that a black cat ran onto the field during the miracle Mets 1969 run, supposedly snarling at Cubs manager Leo Durocher to doom his squad, that Mookie Wilson hit a ground ball through Bill Buckner's legs to crush Boston's World Series dreams, and where the Yankees in 2000 won the first Subway series since the 1950s.

The Stadium, originally to be called Flushing Meadows Park, was instead named after the lawyer who led the effort to bring the Mets to New York, returning National League baseball to New York after the departure of the Dodgers and the Giants in 1957.

William Alfred Shea christened the stadium with two bottles of water—one from the water near Ebbets Field, the Dodgers' old home, and one from the Harlem River near the Polo Grounds, where the Giants had played (and the Mets spent their first two seasons.)

Its four decks are plain, and its outfield symmetrical, with a large scoreboard anchoring right field. It is regarded as a pitchers' park, in part because of the poor visibility for batters. Shea has been renovated, if only slightly. Luxury suits were added after the 1985 season and the exterior was painted Mets blue in 1987. Original plans left open the possibility of enclosing the stadium and seating as many as 90,000.

The full-time home to the NFL Jets, Shea has also housed the Yankees while their stadium was being renovated, and the NFL Giants. In 1975, for a brief, yet crowded, time, Shea was home to the Mets, Jets, Yankees, and Giants. It has seen a lot more than baseball and football. The Beatles landed in center field by helicopter for one of their two concerts. Pope John Paul II has celebrated mass here. Shea has hosted boxing matches, Ice Capades, and concerts, including Janis Joplin and Jimi Hendrix who played at the 1970 Summer Festival for Peace.

Left: In an era of cookie-cutter parks, Shea Stadium was distinctive not for its architectural features, but for its location below the flight path of New York's La Guardia airport With an average of 1,000 a day, even the players sometimes wore earplugs.
National Baseball Hall of Fame

Right: An exterior view of
Shea Stadium.
Digitalballparks.com

Right: The Shea playing
area from above the plate.
*Photofile/National Baseball
Hall of Fame*

Left and Below: Shea stadium cost $28. million to build, and took much longer than anticipated to complete. Originally expected only to play one season at the Polo Grounds, the Mets had to prolong their stay as Shea took 29 months to construct—from groundbreaking on October 28, 1961, to dedication on April 17, 1964.
Digitalballparks.com

Right: Shea Stadium from the upper deck during the game between the Philadelphia Phillies and the New York Mets on July 13, 2003. The Mets won 4–3. The stadium had been designed to be expanded. However, when plans were drawn up to add seats but cover the stadium with a dome, they had to be scrapped because the engineers said the stadium could collapse under the weight. *Photo by Jerry Driendl/Getty Images*

PHILADELPHIA PHILLIES

CITIZENS BANK PARK

PHILADELPHIA PHILLIES

Address: Pattison Avenue, Philadelphia
Capacity: 43,000
Opening Day: April 12, 2004. Cincinnati Reds 4, Philadelphia Phillies 1
Cost to construct: $346 million
Architect: Ewing Cole Cherry Brott (ECCB) and HOK
Dimensions (ft):
Left Field—329
Left Center—370
Center Field—401
Right Center—370
Right Field—330
Defining feature: Electronic Liberty Bell set off by home run
Most expensive seat: $40
Cheapest seat: $15

Philadelphia has had the best of ballparks, and the worst of ballparks. Now it has the newest. Citizens Bank Park, scheduled to open in time for the 2004 season, is Philadelphia's edition of a throwback park, said to mimic stately Shibe Park, which was opened before World War I, and Baker Bowl, where the Phillies began playing baseball in the time of Mark Twain.

It is located across the street from Veterans Stadium, the run down cookie-cutter arena where the Phillies spent the last 30 years. The new park was tilted 45 degrees clockwise, in order to frame a panorama of downtown Philadelphia over its center-field wall. It has a natural grass infield and dirt basepaths, as compared to the artificial turf and small sliding pits in the Vet. It contains 20,000 fewer seats, and a concourse that allows fans to watch the action while they are walking around. The seats behind the plate are 10 feet closer than at the old stadium, and about half the seats are located below the concourse.

The outfield was loosely modeled after Shibe Park, which was best remembered for its enormous French Renaissance facade. Red steel, brick, and stone give the exterior a classic feel, and its main entrances are framed by light standards for a grand approach. Rising 50 feet above first, home, and third are glass towers which are illuminated at night.

The field's distinctive shape, with a little lip in left field, is expected to create entertaining bounces. The architects conducted extensive wind studies, measuring ball trajectories and wind velocities which led them to conclude that Citizens Bank Park will be neither a hitter's nor a pitcher's park.

The center-field concession area is dedicated to Philly Hall of Famer and broadcaster Richie Ashburn. Greg "the Bull" Luzinski, who enjoyed many years of glory at the Vet, serves BBQ in Ashburn Alley, as Boog Powell does for Oriole fans at Baltimore's Camden Yards.

A statue of Connie Mack, the great Philadelphia A's player and manager has been brought over from the Vet. And inside the park, bronze statues honoring Phillies legends Mike Schmidt, Steve Carlton, Robin Roberts and Richie Ashburn celebrate the Phillies' past. A lot of emotional farewells were paid to the Vet in its final days, but the field at Citizens Bank Park was declared ready to go after the 2003 season amid high expectations

Right: Philadelphia Phillies pitcher Randy Wolf delivers the first pitch to Cincinatti Reds D'Angelo Jiminez in the new Citizens Bank Ballpark, April 12, 2004.
© Tim Shaffer/Reuters/Corbis

Far Left: The Phillies had played baseball in "The Vet" for thirty-two years when it finally closed at the end of the 2003 season. Players and fans alike were ready to move on. The once-great stadium had seen its best days many years ago.
National Baseball Hall of Fame

Left: The Vet's unique rounded rectangular shape has been the setting for two All-Star Games (1976, 1996) and three World Series (1980, 1983, and 1993).
National Baseball Hall of Fame

SHIBE PARK (1909–70)
Home of the Philadelphia Athletics 1909–54
Home of the Philadelphia Phillies 1938–70

Just as Baltimore's Camden Yards would do eight decades later, Shibe Park touched off a baseball revolution. Steel-and-concrete, aesthetically pleasing, huge, and with attention to detail, the home of the Philadelphia Athletics and then the Phillies was widely imitated. Over the next five years, Ebbets Field, Forbes Field, Wrigley Field, Fenway Park, Braves Field, and Comiskey Park all opened, while still others were redone in concrete and steel. Beyond its distinctive field and enormous confines, Shibe was distinguished by its enormous French Renaissance façade that belied the notion that it was a mere ballpark.

Named in honor of the A's owner Ben Shibe, it was renamed Connie Mack Stadium in 1953. In 1971 the Phillies moved to Veterans Stadium, a park then hailed as modern, built in the mold of parks in St. Louis, Cincinnati and Pittsburgh. By the time of its last game in 2003, it was ridiculed as sterile and among baseball's worst parks.

Far Left: Hall of Famers who wore a Phillies uniform and played at The Vet include Mike Schmidt, Joe Morgan, Tony Perez, and Steve Carlton.
National Baseball Hall of Fame

Left: Roy Campanella (C) scoring during the Dodgers-Phillies game of October 1, 1949 at Shibe Park.
Photo by George Silk//Time Life Pictures via Getty Images

NATIONAL LEAGUE CENTRAL

The teams of the National League Central are among baseball's oldest. Baseball has been played in Chicago, Cincinnati, Pittsburgh, and St. Louis since the 19th century. However, the division's ballparks are among the game's newest.

Chicago's Wrigley Field, opened in 1916, is the National League's oldest park, and in the eyes of many purists, baseball's best. The manual scoreboard, outfield wall ivy, and close confines have come to define the game. Seventy-five years after Wrigley was built, four National League Central division teams opened 21st century parks.

The Houston Astros replaced their fully enclosed Astrodome with a downtown, retractable-dome stadium in 2000. Pittsburgh moved into a new ball yard on the banks of the Allegheny River that some claim is every bit as pleasant as Wrigley. Milwaukee also opened a new park in 2001, replacing County Stadium, while Cincinnati moved from sterile Riverfront Stadium, later named Cinergy Field, to a new home in 2003. Not to be outdone, the St. Louis Cardinals are building a new stadium in time for the 2006 season, leaving Wrigley Field as the division's only 20th century park.

Right: View of the Great American Ball Park from home plate upper level during the game between the Cincinnati Reds and the Houston Astros.
Photo by Jerry Driendl/Getty Images

CHICAGO CUBS

WRIGLEY FIELD

CHICAGO CUBS

Aka: Weeghman Park (1914–15)
Aka: Cubs Park(1916–26)
Address:
1060 West Addison
Chicago, IL 60613
Capacity: 38,902
Opening day: April 23, 1914—Chicago Federals 9, Kansas City Packers 1
Opening day: (Cubs) April 20, 1916—Chicago Cubs 7, Cincinnati Reds 6 (11 innings)
Cost to construct: $250,000
Architect: Zachary Taylor Davis
Dimensions (ft):
Left Field—355
Left Center—368
Center Field—400
Right Center—368
Right Field—353
Defining feature: Outfield ivy
Little-known ground rule: Baseball stuck in vines covering bleacher wall: Double
Most expensive seat: $45
Cheapest seat: $12
World Series: 1918, 1929, 1932, 1935, 1938, 1945
All-Star Game: 1947, 1962, 1990

Memorable moments:
1917 May 2—Chicago's Jim "Hippo" Vaughn and Cincinnati's Fred Toney both pitch 9 innings of no-hit ball, before Cincinnati's Jim Thorpe drives in the winning run in the 10th inning.
1922 August 25—Cubs beat Phillies 26–23 in Major League Baseball's highest scoring game.
1930 September 28—Hack Wilson drives home his 191st RBI in a 13–11 Cubs win over the Reds, setting a record that still stands.
October 1, 1932. Babe Ruth gestures toward the center field bleachers in the 5th inning of game three of World Series before hitting the ball there for his second home run of the game.
1938 September 28—Gabby Hartnett's "Homer in the Gloamin" beats Pittsburgh to give the Cubs their third consecutive National League pennant.
1970 May 12—Ernie Banks hits his 500th career homer.
1988 May 8—The first night game is played at Wrigley Field. The game against the Phillies is called for rain in the fourth inning. The first official Wrigley night game is played the following night, when the Cubs beat the Mets 6–4.
1998 May 6—20-year-old rookie Kerry Wood strikes out 20 Astros in his fifth major-league start.
1998 September 13—Sammy Sosa hits home runs No. 61 and No. 62 to tie and then eclipse Roger Maris' single-season record, one week after Mark McGwire had done the same.
2003 October 14—With the Cubs leading 3 to 0 and just five outs from their first World Series appearance in 58 years, a Cub fan reaches for a foul ball down the third base line, depriving left fielder Moises Alou a chance to make a catch. The Florida Marlins go on to score eight runs and win the pennant the next night.

Wrigley Field is what every baseball park wants to be.

Simple, intimate, handsome, and distinct, cities and team owners around the country have spent hundreds of millions of dollars, hired architects, engineers, and historians, all hoping to recreate what has existed on Chicago's North side for nearly a century.

Built on the grounds of a seminary in 1914, the park opened as Weeghman Park, home to the Chicago Federals (also known as the Whales) in the soon-to-be defunct Federal League. Two years later it was Cubs Park, when the National League team moved in, and then Wrigley Field when the chewing gum magnate took control of the team a decade later.

Change marked Wrigley's early years. A second deck was added in 1927. The signature bleachers and 27-foot high scoreboard were built in 1937. That same year, Bill Veeck planted hundreds of Boston Ivy plants along the outfield brick wall. A clock was added atop the scoreboard four years later. Since then, time has essentially stood still inside the "friendly confines" which Hack Wilson, Ernie Banks, Billy Williams, Fergie Jenkins, Ryne Sandberg, and Sammy Sosa have all called home.

Take a look at a picture of Wrigley in the early 1940s and another from today. The top hats and black jackets have been replaced by bright blue Cubbie caps and t-shirts and the high rises beyond center field have grown taller, but little else has changed. There were no billboards inside the park then, and there are none today. The scoreboard is still hand-operated (and not large enough to accommodate every out-of-town game since the major leagues expanded.) After each Cub victory, a white flag with a blue W is raised high above the scoreboard, a white L on a blue flag indicates a loss, a system originally created to let Wrigley's neighbors keep track of their team long before the advent of sports tickers or ESPN.

Chicago baseball in the 21st century is much as it was prior to World War II, providing an incredible link to another era and one that ballparks from Baltimore to Seattle have tried to capture for themselves.

Wrigley Field, as the second oldest major-league park after Fenway, is the birthplace of many baseball traditions. It was the first place that allowed fans to keep balls hit into the stands. The first concession stands were built in the park's opening year, after patrons complained that roaming vendors were blocking their view. In 1941, the Cubs became the first team to play organ music in its ballpark. It is here that Harry Caray, leaning outside his broadcast booth with microphone in hand and beer poorly concealed behind the window, made famous the tradition of singing *Take Me Out To The Ballgame* during the seventh inning stretch which is now imitated wherever baseball is played.

Until 1988, Wrigley's most distinctive feature was its lack of lights. Team owners were ready to install them in time for the 1942 season when the U.S. was attacked at Pearl Harbor. The day after the attack, team owner P.K. Wrigley donated the equipment to the War Department. Lights were finally erected in 1988 after league officials threatened to hold Cubs postseason games at the home of the rival Cardinals in St. Louis.

Wrigley's first night game, in what some saw as an omen, was suspended in the fourth inning after a torrential downpour. The first official game was played the following night when the Cubs beat the Mets 6 to 4.

After thousands of games, no baseball has yet hit the center-field scoreboard, though a towering home run hit onto Sheffield Avenue by Bill Nicholson in 1948, and another one hit onto Waveland Avenue in 1959 by Roberto Clemente, barely missed. Sam Snead reached the scoreboard with a golf ball, prior to a game in 1951.

Cub fans are familiar with many smaller changes over the years. Luxury boxes have been added to bring in revenue, and in 1970 a basket was installed along the bleachers to keep fans from interfering with balls. Seats have been erected on the rooftops along Waveland and Sheffield Avenues, where more casual viewing was once a tradition.

Yet Wrigley baseball looks much the same today as it did when Zip Zabel came in to pitch 18 innings in relief over Brooklyn in 1915, when Stan Musial collected his 3,000 hit, when Ernie Banks hit his 512th and final home run, when Fergie Jenkins pitched his 3,000 strikeout, and when Pete Rose tied Ty Cobb with hit No. 4,191.

For all Wrigley has witnessed, it has never seen a Cubs World Series celebration. As one of the league's most dominant teams in the first half of the 20th century, the Cubs brought the World

Series to Wrigley six times between 1918 and 1945, losing each time. The Cubs' last championship team was in 1908, well before there was a ballpark at the corner of Addison and Sheffield.

Above: An undated photo showing Wrigley prior to the 1937 season when its signature bleachers were constructed. The alterations and enhancements made it one of the most pleasant places on earth to watch a ballgame.
National Baseball Hall of Fame

Above: Wrigley Field from a right field skybox across the street from the ballpark during the game between the Phillies and the Cubs on July 23, 2003.
Photo by Jerry Driendl/Getty Images

Right: An aerial view of Wrigley Field. Easy to see why even the players refer to this classic park as the "Friendly Confines." By the time this photo was taken the bleachers and a second level of seats had been added to meet the fan demand.
National Baseball Hall of Fame

Right: Wrigley Field's center-field scoreboard during the game between the Phillies and the Cubs on July 23, 2003. *Photo by Jerry Driendl/Getty Images*

Inset: The ivy and score-board were introduced to Wrigley Field by Bill Veeck in 1937. *National Baseball Hall of Fame*

Right: A packed Wrigley Field seen from the left-field stands.
Digitalballparks.com

Far Right: The Florida Marlins celebrate their 9–6 win over the Chicago Cubs during game seven of the National League Championship series October 15, 2003.
Brian Bahr/Getty Images

Far Right, Inset: Cubs' bleacher band, seen at Wrigley Field.
Digitalballparks.com

Right: The Great American Ball Park from home plate upper level during a National League game between the Cincinnati Reds and the Houston Astros.
Photo by Jerry Driendl/Getty Images

The Great American Ball Park and the Cincinnati night skyline. The suspension bridge is the Roebling Suspension Bridge, erected in 1866 as the Covington and Cincinnati Bridge and renamed after its designer John A. Roebling. *Photo by Jerry Driendl/Getty Images*

Above: Aerial view of the then Riverfront Stadium. It would be renamed Cinergy Field in 1996 after Cincinnati's electric company paid $6 million for the privilege.
National Baseball Hall of Fame

Left: Spectators aboard boats floating on the Ohio River watch as Cinergy Field is imploded on December 29, 2002, to make room for the nearby Great American Ballpark (on the right). More than 1,200lb of explosive material was used.
Photo by Mike Simons/Getty Images

HOUSTON ASTROS

MINUTE MAID PARK

HOUSTON ASTROS

Aka: Enron Field 2000-2002
Address:
501 Crawford Street
Houston, TX 77002
Capacity: 40,950
Opening day: April 7, 2000—Philadelphia Phillies 4, Houston Astros 1
Cost to construct: $248 million
Architect: HOK Sports
Dimensions (ft):
Left Field—315
Left Center—362
Center Field—435
Right Center—373
Right Field—326
Defining feature: Centerfield hill
Most expensive seat: $40
Cheapest seat: $5
World Series: none
All-Star Game: 2004

Memorable moments:
2001 July 18—Jeff Bagwell hits for the cycle as Houston beats St. Louis 17–11.
2001 October 4—Barry Bonds ties Mark McGwire's single season home run record, hitting No. 70 into the second deck.

To appreciate the Astros' new home, think of the Houston Astrodome. Minute Maid Park is the opposite.

The Astrodome was a dark, completely enclosed, oversized gymnasium where power hitters went to die. Minute Maid Field is light, open, thoroughly unique, and conducive to scoring runs. Even when the retractable roof is closed, 50,000 square feet of glass panels allow patrons to gaze upon the Houston skyline or tropical storms passing above.

In its time, the Astrodome represented an amazing architectural achievement, allowing Houston fans to watch their team despite the swampy heat and mosquitoes of summer. Over time, it came to represent everything that modern baseball parks try to avoid.

Now, the Astros play in a state-of-the art structure where the roof alone cost about twice what it took to build the Astrodome. This is no cookie-cutter gymnasium. Its most unusual quirk, Tal's Hill —named after team president Tal Smith —is a grassy knoll in dead center field, that rises at a 20 degree angle to a height of about five feet,

prompting the most graceful centerfielders to watch their feet as they chase down deep fly balls. On the left side of the incline is a flagpole, which is in play as at the old Tiger Stadium.

The left field bleachers are close, just 315 feet away, and protrude into the outfield, creating funny bounces and fantastic views. A one-of-a-kind porch hangs out over the outfield action, where walls come in several different shapes and heights. Small foul territories bring fans close to the field.

The park's signature feature is a 57-foot, 24-ton, 1860s steam locomotive, which chugs down an 800-foot track along the left field roof when the Astros do something special. Trains are a motif throughout the stadium. Most fans enter through the 1911 vintage Union Station, which forms the park's main entrance. The scoreboard is baseball's biggest, and explodes in celebration of every Astros' home run.

The park opened as Enron Field, after the Houston-based energy conglomerate which paid $100 million for 30 years of naming rights. At the park's opener, with soon-to-be President

Bush on hand, Enron President Ken Lay threw out the ceremonial first pitch. Two years later, the energy conglomerate had gone bankrupt amid scandal. The large Enron sign remained on the park until the Astros bought back the naming right. Months later, they sold the rights to Minute Maid.

Right: Enron Field became Minute Maid Park for the 2003 season after an accounting scandal bankrupted the Houston-based energy conglomerate. This photograph shows off well Tal Hill at Minute Maid Park; note also the flagpole, which is in play.
National Baseball Hall of Fame

Left: Aerial view of Enron Field and downtown Houston.
Photo by: Bob Daemmrich/Corbis

Opposite: Minute Maid Park-view toward first base from third base. *Digitalballparks.com*

Left: This photograph of Minute Maid Park affords a view of the 57-foot, 24-ton full-size replica steam loco that runs on an 800-foot track above left field. The park has a strong railway connection: the main entrance is the 1911 Union Station. *Digitalballparks.com*

Astrodome (1965–99)

The Houston Astrodome was hailed as the eighth wonder of the world when it opened, an architectural achievement that would change baseball's relationship to the elements. During the dome's 35-year baseball history, the Astros were rained out once, a enormous 1968 storm which didn't dampen the field, but prevented fans and the umpiring crew from making it to the park. Like a giant gymnasium, the Astrodome provoked awe in visitors who had never imagined indoor baseball, or an animated scoreboard with dancing figures for entertainment.

The Astrodome's field was originally grass, but the transparent roof created a menacing glare. The darkened panes killed the grass, and prompted the need for Astroturf, which become a standard for many other sports venues. Besides baseball, the Astrodome was host to musicians including the Rolling Stones, boxing matches, tennis tournaments, and the 1992 Republican National Convention.

Left: Aerial view of the Houston Astrodome, photographed in 2000. Photo by Paul S. *Howell/Getty Images*

Right: The Houston Astrodome was the home of the Astros for 35 years 1965–2000. *National Baseball Hall of Fame*

Left: A view of the Houston Astrodome during a game between the Chicago Cubs and the Houston Astros on August 29, 1996. The Cubs won the game 4–3.
Getty Images

Right: Houston Astrodome opening night of April 9, 1965, playing the Yankees in an exhibition game in front of President Lyndon B. Johnson.
National Baseball Hall of Fame

MILWAUKEE BREWERS

MILLER PARK

MILWAUKEE BREWERS:

Address:
One Brewers Way
Milwaukee, WI 53214
Capacity: 42,400
Opening Day: April 6, 2001—Milwaukee Brewers 5, Cincinnati Reds 4
Cost to construct: $400 million
Architect: HKS, Inc. (Dallas), NBBJ (L.A.), Eppstein Uhen Architects (Milwaukee)
Dimensions (ft):
Left Field—344
Left Center—370
Center Field—400
Right Center—374
Right Field—345
Defining feature: Bernie Brewer
Most expensive seat: $75
Cheapest seat: $1
World Series: None
All-Star Game: 2002

Memorable momentsÚ
2001 April 6—President Bush throws out the ceremonial first pitch, and the Brewers rally behind Richie Sexson's eighth-inning home run to beat the Cincinnati Reds in Miller Park's debut.
2002 May 23—Dodger outfielder Shawn Green hits four home runs, seven RBI, scores six runs and sets a major-league record with 19 total bases.
2002 July 10—The American and National leagues battle to a 7–7 All-Star game tie. Baseball Commissioner, former Brewer owner, and Milwaukee native Bud Selig is booed for 30 minutes after announcing that the game would not continue because both teams had run out of pitchers.
2003 July 9—Pittsburgh outfielder Randall Simon is lead away in handcuffs after belting a costumed, 19-year-old woman participating in the sixth inning sausage race, with a baseball bat.

After playing for 30 years in County Stadium, a ballpark as plain as its name, the Brewers opened the new millennium in a park with all the latest bells and whistles.

Miller Park is the major leagues' latest retractable dome stadium, this one built in a unique fan shape, in which the 12,000-ton roof pivots around a point near home plate, covering more than 10 acres, and able to open and shut in just over 10 minutes.

The convertible structure not only means year-round climate control in a northern climate where April and September are pushing the baseball envelope, it also strikes wonder in the upper Midwest cheeseheads, who shattered attendance records in the park's first year. During the opening season, fans stuck around after the game on nice summer nights to watch the roof close to the symphonic sounds of Johann Strauss' "Blue Danube Waltz."

The stadium took almost five years to build, opening a year late after a tragic crane accident in 1999 killed three steel workers, and added $100 million to the project's cost.

The roof stands more than 30 stories high at its peak, adding an imposing new landmark to Milwaukee's modest skyline. The Brewers claim on their internet site, rather oddly, that the stadium weighs the equivalent of 62.5 million bowling balls, and that it would take 4.66 billion baseballs to fill it top to bottom.

Architects boast that the roof's steel mirrors the bridges over the Menomonee River, though the height of the walls and the omnipresence of the dome has led fans to complain that it feels like an indoor stadium even when the roof is open.

Patrons in County Stadium got to watch the project from their seats, as it was built just beyond centerfield in what was a parking lot. It includes a manual scoreboard and seats close to the field in the vain of other recent parks. Brewer Hall of Famer Robin Yount helped design the park's dimensions, which includes a quirky outfield with unique slants and angles.

Outside is a classic brick facade, with statues of Yount and Hank Aaron.

The Brewers transplanted some of their most distinctive traditions from County Stadium, including Bernie Brewer, who used to slide down an enormous, several-story high slide into a beer stein, and now does the same onto a platform in left field. Humans dressed in sausage costumes race around the bases in the middle of the sixth inning. And huge parking lots facilitate Wisconsin's obsession with tailgate parties.

Outside, eight names have been immortalized on a "Walk of Fame," that encircles the ballpark plaza, including Aaron, Yount, Rollie Fingers, Cecil Cooper, Paul Molitor, Allan H. (Bud) Selig, Harry Dalton and Bob Uecker.

The stadium offers $1 "Ueker seats," named after the well known Brewer's broadcaster, obstructed by roof pivots and located in the upper deck terrace, but still one of the best deals in baseball.

Right: A view of the entrance to Miller Park before the game between the Milwaukee Brewers and the Cincinnati Reds on May 17, 2003. The Brewers defeated the Reds 8–6.
Photo by Jonathan Daniel/Getty Images

This Page: Miller Park during the game between the Milwaukee Brewers and the Cincinnati Reds on May 17, 2003. The Brewers defeated the Reds 8–6.
Photo by Jonathan Daniel/Getty Images

Opposite, Left: Kazuhiro Sasaki of the Seattle Mariners and his son Shogo take in the media during batting practice for the MLB All-Star Game and MLB All-Star Home Run Derby July 8, 2002, at Miller Park.
Photo by Matthew Stockman/Getty Images

Opposite, Right: Mascot Bernie Brewer of the Milwaukee Brewers looks on from "Bernie's Dugout" during the game against the Cincinnati Reds at Miller Park on May 17, 2003. The Brewers defeated the Reds 8–6.
Photo by Jonathan Daniel/Getty Images

MILWAUKEE COUNTY STADIUM (1953-2000)

Home of the Milwaukee Braves (1953-1965)
Home of the Milwaukee Brewers (1970-2000)

Unless you count the man who slid into a beer stein after each Brewer home run, there were few frills at Milwaukee County Stadium. The straight-forward ball-park was made exclusively for baseball, and the fans who sang "Beer Barrel Polka" during the seventh-inning stretch rarely com-plained. It is here that Hank Aaron started his remarkable career, and where Warren Spahn enjoyed nine, 20-win seasons.

County Stadium was home to the Braves when they moved from Boston in 1953, and was a National League park for 13 seasons until their departure for Atlanta 13 years later. The American League Brewers moved in before the 1970 season (and 27 years before their return to the National League.)

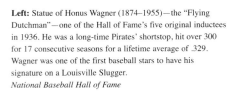

Left: Statue of Honus Wagner (1874–1955)—the "Flying Dutchman"—one of the Hall of Fame's five original inductees in 1936. He was a long-time Pirates' shortstop, hit over 300 for 17 consecutive seasons for a lifetime average of .329. Wagner was one of the first baseball stars to have his signature on a Louisville Slugger.
National Baseball Hall of Fame

Below: PNC Park in Pittsburgh, Pennsylvania during the game between the New York Mets and the Pittsburgh Pirates on April 1, 2001.
Photo by Jamie Squire/Allsport via Getty Images

Opposite: Aerial of PNC Park looking over the Allegheny River.
National Baseball Hall of Fame

Left: On May 25, 1935, Babe Ruth hit the last home run of his major-league career in Forbes Field. The blast cleared the right-field wall, then cleared the screen and finally cleared the doubledeck grandstands. The historic shot (a first of that distance in Forbes Field) was approximately eighty-six feet high and at least three-hundred feet away from home plate. *National Baseball Hall of Fame*

Right: View over the Forbes Field diamond. Known for its sheer size, the park was abandoned in favor of Three-Rivers Stadium, a cookie cutter park built at a cost of $40 million. *Time Life Pictures/Getty Images*

FORBES FIELD (1909–70)

Forbes Field was among baseball's first luxury stadiums. Built beside one of the city's most upscale neighborhoods, it boasted elevators, electric lights, telephones, and even toilets for its patrons. The field was distinguished by its sheer size, which spread 376 feet to right field and 462 to dead center. The distance from home plate to the backstop was well over 100 feet, about double today's standard, frustrating generations of foul ball hitters.

The park was named after John Forbes, a general in the British Army who captured Fort Duquesne during the French and Indian War. Home to Honus Wagner, Ralph Kiner and Roberto Clemente, its most storied moment came in the bottom of the ninth inning during the final game of the World Series between the Pirates and the Yankees, when Bill Mazeroski hit a series ending ball high over the left-field wall. Part of the outfield wall remains on the University of Pittsburgh campus where the stadium once stood. The park was abandoned in 1970, in favor of ultra-modern, Three Rivers Stadium.

Right: Forbes Field was
remarkably well-laid out,
with landscaped gardens and
statues
*National Baseball Hall of
Fame*

FORBES FIELD
LAST OUT
6/28/70

Left: The last game at
Forbes Field on June 28,
1970.
*National Baseball Hall of
Fame*

ST. LOUIS CARDINALS

BUSCH STADIUM

ST. LOUIS CARDINALS

Address:
250 Stadium Plaza
St. Louis, MO 63102
Capacity: 49,814
Opening day: May 12, 1966—St. Louis Cardinals 4, Atlanta Braves 3 (12 innings)
Cost to construct: $55 million
Architect: Sverdrup & Parcel and Associates
Dimensions (ft):
Left Field—330
Left Center—372
Center Field—402
Right Center—372
Right Field—330
Defining feature: Stadium roof's 96 arches
World Series: 1967, 1968, 1982, 1985, 1987
All-Star Game: 1966

Memorable moments:
1968 October 2—Bob Gibson strikes out 17 Tigers en route to a 4–0 victory over Denny McLain in a matchup of soon-to-be MVP winners in the first game of the World Series.
1969 September 15—Steve Carlton strikes out 19 Mets, but loses after Ron Swoboda hits a pair of two-run homers to lead the Mets over the Reds 4–3.
1974 September 11—Cards beat Mets 4–3 in 25 innings, the longest game in major-league history. About 1,000 fans are still in their seats when the game ends at 3:13 a.m.
1974 September 10—Lou Brock steals base Nos. 104 and 105 to set new single-season record.
1979 August 13—Lou Brock collects his 3,000th career hit off the Cubs Dennis Lamp in the fourth inning.
1985 October 13—Cardinal Rookie sensation Vince Coleman gets his leg trapped in the stadium's automated tarpaulin as it unrolls across the infield prior to a National League playoff game, ending his season.
1985 October 14—Shortstop Ozzie Smith homers off Dodgers Tom Niedenfuer in the bottom of the ninth inning to beat the Dodgers in a dramatic playoff victory. It is the first home run he has ever hit in from the left side of the plate.
1998 September 8—Mark McGwire hits home run No. 62, breaking Roger Maris record.. He hits Nos. 69 and 70 on September 27.

When baseball elitists talk about a "cookie-cutter" stadium, they are talking about Busch Stadium.

Pittsburgh's Three Rivers Stadium, Philadelphia's Veterans Stadium, and Cincinnati's Riverfront Stadium also fit the description. But those stadiums each came after St. Louis set the mold, and all of them have already been replaced.

Busch Stadium was built in 1966, opening just six months after the city's Gateway Arch on the banks of the Mississippi several blocks away. It was the pride of a bygone era. The stadium was perfectly round, the field exactly symmetrical. The walls were uniform height, the three decks exactly alike. It was made for football as well as baseball. It was concrete, antiseptic and sterile.

And for baseball purists, it got worse. Artificial turf replaced the natural grass after four seasons. Seven years later, they carpeted the entire infield, leaving dirt only in a small sliding pit around the bases. But St. Louis is a devoted baseball city, and it adjusted. The far-away foul poles and long power alleys favored pitchers and

speedsters, and Hall of Famers like Bob Gibson, and Lou Brock, and Curt Flood thrived. In its first two decades, Busch stadium hosted five World Series.

The stadium kept improving through the 1990s. In 1992, the fences were lowered and brought a few feet closer to the plate. In 1996, grass replaced the artificial turf. In 1997, a hand-operated scoreboard was constructed in center-field, and a visitors' bullpen added to right field. The departure of the NFL's Cardinals to Arizona meant Busch was for baseball only, and suddenly it had turned into a much nicer park.

The 96 open arches that encircle the field just below the roof mimic the 60-story Gateway Arch outside, and provide views for those along the left field side. The arches also distinguish Busch from other stadiums built in its era, as do the red seats and the sea of patrons who drape themselves in the team colors.

Busch was one of the first stadiums to be located directly downtown, built as part of an urban renewal project (the National Bowling Hall of Fame is across the street.)

Outside, bronze statues of Stan Musial, Bob Gibson, Lou Brock, Enos Slaughter, Red Schoendienst, Dizzy Dean, Rogers Hornsby, George Sisler, and Jack Buck encircle the stadium to pay tribute to the Cardinals' past.

Opposite: View over third to first base showing off the clear, unobstructed, views afforded by this nearly 40-year-old structure. *Digitalballparks.com*

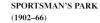

Left: External view of Busch Stadium. With a diameter of more than 800 feet, the stadium covers more than 12 acres. *Digitalballparks.com*

Below: Dusk view of Busch Stadium; just visible over the stand is the St Louis Gateway Arch. The Cardinals announced on December 23, 2003, that they have all the necessary funding in place to begin work immediately on building a new ballpark in downtown St. Louis. The new stadium will be ready for the start of the 2006 season. Fans were invited to attend the ceremonial groundbreaking on January 17. *Digitalballparks.com*

Left: Busch Stadium and the St Louis Gateway Arch, designed by Eero Saarinen. It commemorates Thomas Jefferson and the nation's expansion west. *National Baseball Hall of Fame*

SPORTSMAN'S PARK (1902–66)
Home of the St. Louis Browns (AL) 1902-1953
Home of the St. Louis Cardinals (NL) 1920-1966

Baseball has been played on the corner of Grand and Dodier since 1871. It was in 1902 that Sportsman's Park was built, which boasts more major-league games than any park in history. For a remarkable 34 years, the stadium was home to both the Browns of the American League and the Cardinals of the National League. The two teams met in the 1944 World Series, with the Cardinals, the more dominant team during most of their joint history, coming out on top.

This is the park where Rogers Hornsby and Stan Musial played, where a goat in the 1940s helped the grounds crew keep the grass trim; where a midget was sent up by team owner Bill Veeck to draw a walk. It was also the last park in the majors to exclude African Americans from its general admission, providing them seats in the 1940s in a right field pavilion, which was screened so no home run balls could enter.

The Browns left for Baltimore in 1953, and the Cardinals moved into Busch Stadium after the 1966 season. The grandstands are gone, but baseball is still played on the field where Sportsman's once stood.

Right: A panoramic view of Busch Stadium and nearby skyscrapers in St. Louis, Missouri.
Photo by: Joseph Sohm; ChromoSohm Inc./CORBIS

NATIONAL LEAGUE WEST

The National League West includes two of baseball's most storied franchises, the Giants (1880s) and the Dodgers (1890s), who, like so many Americans, left their New York homes in the late 1950s for California. The remaining three teams are relative babes—the Padres born in the 1960s, the Rockies in the 1980s, and the Diamondbacks in the 1990s.

The ballparks of the National League West have distinction. In SBC Park, sluggers hit the ball into the San Francisco Bay. In Phoenix's Bank One Ballpark, they can hit the ball into a right field swimming pool. In San Diego's PETCO Park, batters smash balls off a left field warehouse, while in Denver's Coors Field, they take advantage of the thin, mile-high air.

Los Angeles' Dodger Stadium, opened in 1962, is the division's only park built before 1995, and is still regarded as one of the best places in the division to watch a baseball game. The National League West is the only division in baseball where there is no talk of any team building a new park for many years to come.

Left: A general view of Coors Field prior to the National League game between the Arizona Diamondbacks and the Colorado Rockies on June 30, 2003. The Diamondbacks defeated the Rockies 8–7 in 12 innings.
Photo by Brian Bahr/Getty Images

ARIZONA DIAMONDBACKS
BANK ONE BALLPARK

ARIZONA DIAMONDBACKS

Address:
401 E. Jefferson Street
Phoenix, AZ 85004
Capacity: 49,033
Opening day: March 31, 1998—Colorado Rockies 9,
Arizona Diamondbacks 2
Cost to construct: $354 million
Architect: Ellerbe Becket
Dimensions (ft):
Left Field—330
Left Center—374
Center Field—407
Right Center—374
Right Field—334
Defining feature: Right field swimming pool
Most expensive seat: $60
Cheapest seat: $1
World Series: 2001
All-Star Game: None

Memorable moments:
1999 July 11—Jay Bell hits a grand slam in the sixth
   inning, winning $1 million for fan Gylene Hoyle,
   who had predicted the player and the inning in a
   pre-game contest.
2001 May 8—Randy Johnson strikes out 20 Reds to tie a
   major-league record, yet does not record a win.
   The Diamondbacks ultimately triumph 4–3 in 11
   innings.
2001 October 28—The Diamondbacks beat the Yankees
   4–0 to take a two games to none lead in the World
   Series as Randy Johnson throws a three-hit, complete game shutout.
2001 November 4—Luis Gonzalez hits a bases-loaded
   single to score Jay Bell, capping a two-run, ninth-
   inning comeback to beat the Yankees 3–2 in the
   seventh game of the World Series.

Bank One Ballpark is a monument to the power of air conditioning.

The very qualities that make the Phoenix area such a popular destination for Cactus League games in the spring make it downright unbearable for baseball in the summer, when the average high temperature tops 100 degrees for three consecutive months.

The "BOB" cooled things down with 8,000 tons of air conditioning equipment, capable of creating enough cold air to chill 2,500 homes, and bring temperatures down by 30 degrees in three hours.

The unique retractable roof allows sunlight to shine on the natural turf, while keeping the oppressive desert heat from baking the grandstands. Nine million pounds of structural steel, using the same technology as a drawbridge, can open and close in less than five minutes, and can move into a variety of partially open positions.

With the climate under control, the BOB can focus on baseball. More than 80 percent of the seats are located between the foul poles, and there is no upper deck in the outfield. Natural turf and an old-fashioned dirt path connecting the pitchers mound to home plate, give the park more of a classic feel than might be expected under a dome.

The stadium is cluttered with advertisements, among other distractions. Its most unique feature is the swimming pool and hot tub located just beyond the right field fence about 415 feet from home plate, where bathing suit clad patrons can buys tickets for a swim and a unique outfield view. Chicago's Mark Grace was the first to plunk a ball into the pool in May of 1998, a feat that has since been duplicated dozens of times.

Outside, Bank One Ballpark more resembles an airplane hanger than a baseball stadium. The red brick and green structural steel are said by the architects to blend into Phoenix's surrounding warehouse district, but the huge baseball murals on the side give it the look of a basketball or hockey arena.

Inside, the Diamondbacks boast a quarter mile of concession stands, and enough entertainment to draw 3.6 million fans its opening year. The park hosted the World Series in only its fourth year, beating the Yankees in a dramatic, come-from-behind, ninth-inning rally in game seven.

Right: External view of Bank One Ballpark in Phoenix.
Digitalballparks.com

Following page, Left: Front entrance of the Bank One Ballpark. The $354 million cost of the structure was split between the Diamondback owners (32 percent) and public funding that came from a quarter-cent sales tax in Maricopa County.
Photo by Jeff Carlick /Allsport via Getty Images

Following page, Right: March 31, 1998: a view of batting practice before a game between the Diamondbacks and the Colorado Rockies at Bank One Ballpark. The Rockies defeated the Diamondbacks 9–2.
Photo by Vincent Laforet /Allsport via Getty Images

Left: General Manager Jerry Colangelo of Arizona Diamondbacks throws the ceremonial first pitch before his team plays against the San Diego Padres during Opening Day at Bank One Ballpark April 1, 2002. The Diamondbacks won 2–0. *Photo by Donald Miralle/Getty Images*

Right: Bank One Ballpark boasts a 385 square-foot warm water pool and an 85 square-foot hot tub. *Digitalballparks.com*

COLORADO ROCKIES

COORS FIELD

COLORADO ROCKIES

Address:
2001 Blake Street
Denver, CO 80205
Capacity: 50,544
Opening day: April 26, 1995—Colorado Rockies 11, New York Mets 9 (14 innings)
Cost to construct: $215 million
Architect: HOK Sports
Dimensions (ft):
Left Field—347
Left Center—390
Center Field—415
Right Center—375
Right Field—350
Defining feature: Row of purple, mile-high seats
Most expensive seat: $45
Cheapest seat: $1
World Series: None
All-Star Game: 1998

Memorable moments:
1995 April 26—Dante Bichette christens the park with a 14th-inning, three-run home run, to beat the New York Mets 11–9 in the opening game.
1995 October 1—The Rockies beat the Giants 10–9 to win a spot in the National League playoffs in just their third season.
1996 September 12—Ellis Burks steals his 30th base of the season, a month after hitting his 30th home run, to join baseball's elite 30–30 club. Teammate Dante Bichette joins him by hitting his 30th home run the following night.
1999 May 19—The Reds beat the Rockies 24–12 in the third highest scoring game since the turn of the century.
1998 July 7—The American League beats the National League 13–8 in the highest scoring All-Star game in history.
2001 September 9—Giants Barry Bonds hits home runs No. 61, 62, and 63 en route to his record 73-home run season..
2003 April 10—First baseman Todd Helton snags a line drive off the bat of Cardinal Orlando Palmeiro, setting in motion the Rockies first triple play.

The purple seats on the 20th row of Coors Field's upper deck tell the story of this ballpark. It is there that the elevation reaches 5,280 feet, exactly one mile above sea level. At that altitude balls fly further. Curve balls break less sharply. And that, more than any other feature, has defined the Rockies' home.

Coors Field, the first park in the National League to be constructed exclusively for baseball since Dodger Stadium 33 years earlier, is by no means a small park. Its center field fence is a deep 415 feet, and left center juts out nine feet deeper. Yet the dimensions are deceptive. According to a team estimate, a ball hit 400 feet at sea-level Yankee Stadium would travel 440 feet in mile high Coors Field. The thin air contributed to a record-setting 1999 season, when teams combined for an average of 15 runs and four home runs each game.

The incredible offense, the classic charm of the old-fashioned park, and the views of the Rocky Mountains in the distance, have made Coors Field among the best attended parks in baseball history.

The deep red brick and Colorado sandstone exterior makes Coors Field look like it has always been located in Denver's lower downtown, on a spot where a train depot once stood. The classic architecture and old fashioned corner front clock are reminiscent of Ebbets Field, and anchor a newly bustling downtown neighborhood.

Inside, the triple deck structure features small foul areas, an asymmetric field, and seats with sight lines geared toward the infield. A heating system under the field melts snow quickly, and its drainage system can clear away five inches or rain in a matter of hours.

The absence of an upper deck in left field provides fans along the first base and right field side a spectacular view of the Rocky Mountains. The stadium's designers passed up the chance to offer a panoramic view of downtown Denver so the sun would not be in batters' eyes, though the skyline is still visible from the top of the Rockpile, a 2,300-seat center field bleacher section where many tickets are held until game day, and kids and seniors can get in for just $1.

The park was originally designed to be even more intimate, seating just 43,000. But the huge popularity of baseball in nearby Mile High Stadium, where the Rockies played their first two years, persuaded the owners to add another 6,000 seats.

Right: A view of the baseball diamond during the game between the St. Louis Cardinals and the Colorado Rockies at Coors Field on July 25, 1999. The Cardinals defeated the Rockies 10-6.
Photo by Brian Bahr/Allsport via Getty Images

220

Left: A view toward the diamond and downtown Denver taken during a game between the Atlanta Braves and Colorado Rockies on June 18, 1995. A row of purple seats in the upper deck mark the elevation at exactly one mile above sea level.
Photo by Nathan Bilow/Allsport via Getty Images

Right: A view over the diamond toward the Rocky Mountains: Coors Field has wonderful views from its substantial stands.
Photo by Jonathan Daniel/Allsport via Getty Images

LOS ANGELES

DODGER STADIUM

LOS ANGELES

Address:
1000 Elysian Park Avenue
Los Angeles, CA 90012
Capacity: 56,000
Opening Day: April 10, 1962—Cincinnati Reds 6, Los Angeles Dodgers 3
Cost to construct: $23 million
Architect: Emil Praeger
Dimensions:
Left Field—330
Left Center—385
Center Field—395
Right Center—385
Right Field—330
Defining feature: Wavy roof over bleachers
Little-known ground rule: In its first year, the foul poles were mistakenly placed entirely in foul territory, and required special league dispensation to recognize balls that hit them as fair. Home plate was moved the following year to bring the poles into fair territory
World Series: 1963, 1965, 1966, 1974, 1977, 1978, 1981, 1988
All-Star Game: 1980

Memorable moments:
1962 October 3—Giants score four 9th inning runs to beat the Dodgers 6 to 4, winning a best of three playoff and the National League pennant.
1963 October 6—The Dodgers sweep the Yankees in the World Series, despite Whitey Ford's 2-hitter. Frank Howard gets both Dodger hits including a 5th inning home run.
1968 June 4—Don Drysdale blanks Pittsburgh for his sixth consecutive shutout, a major-league record.
1969 August 5—Pirate Willie Stargell hits a home run completely out of Dodger Stadium, a feat he would accomplish twice in his career. No one else has ever hit one out of the park.
1976 April 25—Cubs outfielder Rick Monday grabs an American flag from two fans about to set it on fire during a game.
1981 April 27—20-year-old rookie sensation Fernando Valenzuela blanks the Giants 5 to 0 for his fourth shutout in five starts, while posting an 0.20 ERA and a .438 batting average.
1988 October 15—Hobbling pinch hitter Kirk Gibson hits a two-strike, two-out, two-run homer off Oakland's Dennis Eckersley to win game one of the World Series 5 to 4.
1995 August 10—The Dodgers forfeit a game against the Cardinals on "ball day" after a ninth inning fracas which began when Raul Mondesi and manager Tommy Lasorda are ejected for arguing with the home plate umpire, and ends when hundreds of souvenir balls bombard the umpires and Cardinal players.

Dodger Stadium isn't a "retro" park, nor does it pretend to be.

Five-tiered, perfectly symmetrical, and without a single deep red brick, Dodger Stadium sits atop Chavez Ravine as a testament to West Coast fans' affection for baseball.

At a time when old-fashioned, or neoclassical parks are the rage, Dodger Stadium stands out as the exception that proves there is more than one way to build a great baseball park.

For decades, what distinguished Dodger Stadium was its simplicity, its cleanliness, and its single-minded devotion to the game. Between the opening of Chicago's Wrigley Field in 1914 and Denver's Coors Field in 1995, Dodger Stadium was the only National League park built exclusively for baseball.

Dodger owner Walter O'Malley, who broke Brooklyn's heart by moving the Dodgers west, was given the site by the city of Los Angeles, which then evicted some disgruntled Mexican American residents from the hilltop, creating Latino animosity toward the Dodgers that persisted for decades.

The wayward Angels also played at Dodger Stadium until their park in Anaheim was opened in 1966, preferring to call it Chavez Ravine so as not to advertise their cross town rivals.

Deep power alleys have made this a pitchers' park, and Sandy Koufax, Don Drysdale, Fernando Valenzuela, and Orel Hershiser all thrived here. The grounds keeping is meticulous. More than 3,000 trees cover the 300-acre site, including several dozen trademark palm trees down the right and left field foul lines, which along with the Elysian Hills and the distant San Gabriel Mountains, give the park a distinctive Southern California look. The computer-controlled, Bermuda grass field, with state-of-the art vacuum chambers to assist draining, was rated No. 1 by baseball players in a *Sports Illustrated* survey in 2003.

The sight lines are on the mark, with no obstructed views. Each deck is freshly painted each season with its own color. Spectacular sunsets and the distinctive wavy roof over the bleachers give an instantly recognizable look to the stadium which was originally designed with

the ability to expand to 85,000 seats, but has remained far smaller.

Dodger Stadium has hosted many events. Pope John Paul II celebrated mass there in 1987. The Beatles, the Rolling Stones, and the Three Tenors are among the long list of performers who have played on the field which also hosted Olympic baseball competition, the Harlem Globetrotters, boxing matches, and even a ski-jumping exhibition.

Little has changed over the past four decades. A video screen capable of showing instant replays, that debuted during the 1980 All-Star game, was baseball's first. Since 2000, the Dodgers have added new field level seats, and club suits, and a new state-of-the-art video screen. Dodger fans, drawn by Dusty Baker, Ron Cey, Steve Garvey, Bert Hooton and Tommy John, were the first in the majors to top three million in attendance in 1978, a feat they have since repeated 17 times.

Right: Another sellout
crowd enjoys a game at
Dodger Stadium.
*Photo by: Robert Landau/
CORBIS*

Right: External view of the stadium, showing some of the 3,400 trees planted in the 300-acre site. Dodger Stadium has parking facilities for 16,000 automobiles. *Digitalballparks.com*

Far Right: The classic lines of Ebbets Field seen during the 1956 World Series. *National Baseball Hall of Fame*

EBBETS FIELD
(1913–57)
Home of the Brooklyn Dodgers

Ebbets Field is arguably where baseball
became the national pastime. For 45
years, the stadium between Brooklyn's
Bedford and Flatbush neighborhoods
defined what it meant to go the ballpark. From its brick arched exterior to
its ornate domed rotunda, many of
today's stadiums reflect its memory.
Seats were close to the field. The outfield wall framed a uniquely shaped
field. Its trademark Shaefer Beer billboard flashed an "H" for hits and an
"E" for errors. Clothier Abe Stark
invited players to hit his advertisement
on the outfield fence for a free suit,
something he never needed to pay up.

It was here that Jackie Robinson
broke the color barrier in 1947, where
television broadcast its first game,
where the Dodgers won nine pennants,
and where owner Walter O'Malley
broke Brooklyn's heart by taking his
team to Los Angeles.

In its final years, O'Malley com-
plained that the stadium was falling
apart, and he searched for a new home.
He was not satisfied with the plot of
land offered to him in Queens where
the Mets would end up several years
later. He left Brooklyn for the west
after the 1957 season. The wrecking
balls began demolishing the park in
1960. Today, the site is home to a low-
income housing project, aptly named
the Jackie Robinson apartments.

Left: Opening day for Brooklyn Stadium—that would become Ebbets Field. Rival teams line the diamond as the band plays and a procession nears the home plate where it will sing the national anthem. *Digitalballparks.com*

Right: The Dodgers played their last game at Ebbets Field on September 24, 1947, before moving to the west coast. The stadium was demolished in 1960.

SAN DIEGO PADRES

PETCO PARK

SAN DIEGO PADRES

Address:
100 Park Boulevard, San Diego
CA 92173
Capacity: 46,000
Opening day: April 8, 2004. San Diego Padres 4, San
Francisco Giants 3 (10 innings)
Cost to construct: $449 million
Architect: HOK Sports
Dimensions (ft):
Left Field—334
Left Center—367
Center Field—396
Right Center—387
Right Field—322
Defining feature: Left field Western Metal Supply Co.
Building

Baseball was played in downtown San Diego before there really was a downtown. More than a 130 years later, the bustling city center is home to the nation's newest downtown stadium, just blocks from the spot of the first sandlot games.

PETCO Park is a "retro" stadium with a distinctly Southern California look. Surrounded by jacaranda trees, water walls, natural stone, and a stucco exterior, the park offers panoramic views of downtown skyscrapers, Mission Bay, Balboa Park, and the arid mountains that surround the city.

Its trademark feature is a left-field warehouse, the turn-of-the-century Western Metal Supply Co. building. Though far smaller than Camden Yard's B&O warehouse, it directly abuts the field, creating an irresistible target for right handed hitters. The left corner of the building holds the left-field foul pole, and each of its four floors contains outdoors seating and a unique perspective on the game.

Unlike the Padres' old home at Qualcomm Stadium, also known as Jack Murphy Field,

PETCO Park was built exclusively for baseball. The park is intimate, with 20,000 fewer seats than Qualcomm, three decks rather than four, seats located much closer to the field, and all angled toward the pitchers mound. The park boasts a capacity of 46,000, though there are only 42,000 seats, reflecting a range of standing room options for fans who can see the ballgame from the concourse and a variety of porches and terraces, in addition to the center field "Park at the Park," a grass park and picnic area for about 2,500 fans.

The unusual (and already ridiculed) name comes from the San Diego-based retailer of pet supplies, which bought the naming rights reportedly for $60 million over 22 years.

Outside, where the early sandlot games were played, the ballpark is anchor to a larger downtown redevelopment project, with plans for a new library, museum, and apartments.

Right: The San Diego Padres play against the New York Mets at Petco Park on April 30, 2004.
© David Madison/NewSport/Corbis

Left: Looking across the diamond over third base toward the Qualcomm scoreboard. *Digitalballparks.com*

Right: Exterior of Qualcomm Stadium. It It is still being used by the NFL San Diego Chargers. *Digitalballparks.com*

Following pages: Two more views of Qualcomm Stadium with scoreboard detail. 2003 was the final season for the Padres in Qualcomm Stadium. Constructed in 1967, "the Q" has been Padres' home since their inaugural season in 1969. It has hosted a pair of World Series (1984 and 1998) and a pair of Major League Baseball All-Star games (1978 and 1992). *Digitalballparks.com*

Above Left: Viewed from one of the luxury boxes at SBC Park is McCovey Cove, a splash target for left-handed sluggers throughout the league. The Cove is separated from the right field seats by a promenade, popular with casual fans interested in catching a play or two while passing by on a summer's walk.
Photo by Deanne Fitzmaurice/San Francisco Chronicle

Left: Giants fans fill up McCovey Cove in all manner of water craft whenever slugger Barry Bonds steps up to the plate. Each hopes to catch or at least retrieve a home run souvenir from a game at SBC Park , until the 2004 season, known as Pacific Bell Park. A Bonds at bat is definitely the best chance of doing so. Of the 31 "splash hits" since the park opened in 2001, Barry Bonds has hit 27.
Photo by Carlos Avila Gonzalez/San Francisco Chronicle

Above: The great Giants' slugger, Barry Bonds, walking to the on deck Circle before his first at bat in a game at Pac Bell Park on September 13, 2003.
Photo by Liz Mangelsdorf/San Francisco Chronicle

Right: General view of SBC Park during the national anthem before game three of the National League championship series between the Cardinals and the Giants on October 12, 2002.
Photo by Matthew Stockman /Getty Images

Left: Stand-in Pitcher Kirk Rueter—#46 of the San Francisco Giants—throws a pitch during game five of the National League Championship series against the St. Louis Cardinals on October 14, 2002. The Giants won the game 2–1 and the series 4–1.
Getty Images

Far Left: Fans stand in a moment of silence in a pre-game ceremony in honor of the victims of September 11 before the game between the Dodgers and the Giants at Pacific Bell Park on September 11, 2002. The Dodgers defeated the Giants 7–3.
Getty Images

Right: In recognition of the Hall of Fame player who wore the Giants' number 24 for 22 seasons, this nine-foot bronze statue of the great Willie Mays, welcomes fans to the entrance to the newly renamed SBC Park at 24 Willie Mays Plaza. The 24 palm trees that line the plaza are another part of the tribute to one of baseball's most honored and beloved players.
Photo by Scott Sommerdorf/San Francisco Chronicle

Inset, Right: At 5:04 on October 17, 1989, a 7.1 earthquake struck the San Francisco Bay Area as the Giants and Oakland A's were preparing for game three of that year's World Series. This photo shows the scene at Candlestick Park moments after the quake hit, rattling the press boxes, knocking out power, and prompting a giant roar from the shaken fans. The game was postponed minutes later. The A's went on to sweep the Giants in four games.
Photo by John O'Hara/San Francisco Chronicle

Left: Exterior view of Candlestick park as boats bring fans in for opening day game against St. Louis Casrdinals, April 12, 1960..
Photo by Jon Brenneis/Time Life Pictures/Getty Images

Far Left: General view of Candlestick Park, home of the San Francisco Giants in c. 1989
Photo by Otto Greule Jr/Getty Images

This Page: Views of the Polo Grounds.
National Baseball Hall of Fame

This Page: Interior views of the Polo Grounds.
Associated Press/National Baseball Hall of Fame; Corbis/National Baseball Hall of Fame

Following Page: An aerial view of SBC Park, then known as Pacific Bell Park, framed by the San Francisco skyline as fans arrive about an hour before the first pitch the park's first game ever, an exhibition between the Giants and the Milwaukee Brewers in March of 2000.
Grant Ward/San Francisco Chronicle

INDEX

Far Left: Night view of Qualcomm from above first base.
Digitalballparks.com

Left: Qualcomm's capacity was 67,544 in 1997.
Digitalballparks.com

Below, Inset: Opening day national anthem before the April 1, 1997, game between the New York Mets and San Diego. The Padres won the game 12–5. N
Photo by Jed Jacobsohn/Allsport via Getty Images

SAN FRANCISCO GIANTS

SBC PARK

Ask any five-year old. There is a primal satisfaction that comes from splashing a solid object into a body of water.

The Giants have taken this proposition to major-league heights at SBC Park, where the chilly waters of the San Francisco Bay sit a tantalizing 352 feet from home plate.

There is much that is appealing about the Giants' new home. The park is small and its dimensions intimate. The sight lines are engineered exclusively for baseball. The field is asymmetrical with a 25-foot high brick wall just 309 feet from home plate, the closest foul pole in the majors. The view beyond the outfield is as beautiful an urban landscape as can be imagined.

But for all its charms, nothing compares to the childishly irresistible anticipation that a powerful left handed hitter might clear the 25-foot brick wall in right field, and plop a home run into the water named after the Giants' Hall of Fame first baseman Willie McCovey. The Giants have such a hitter, and SBC is unmistakably the park that (Barry) Bonds built. Just as the Yankees erected a short right-field fence in 1923 for their star left hander, Babe Ruth, the Giants built SBC for Bonds, the marquee power hitter of his time. As the 2004 season opened, only four players had "gone Bay," but Bonds himself has done it 27 times, thrilling capacity crowds who were just warming up after four decades at frigid Candlestick Park.

Just as fans gather on Chicago's Waveland Avenue for the chance at a home run ball, sailors, kayakers, and other boaters fill McCovey Cove during Giants games, their eyes fixed on the right field fence. The location is so close that when the Yankees Jorge Posada hit the ball into the cove during an exhibition game, the ball was scooped up by boater Mike Quinby who promptly threw it back onto the field on a fly.

SBC was built in the mold of Camden Yards. Rather than the B&O warehouse in right field, it is the Bay, with stunning vistas of the East Bay hills and the Bay Bridge from the upper deck. Architects resisted even more sweeping views in order to reduce the wind, and to give Bonds a better shot at reaching the Bay. Temperatures are not nearly as cold as at windy Candlestick, where former Giants pitcher Stu Miller was famously blown off the mound during the 1961 All-Star Game. Still, you won't catch many locals wearing short sleeves at night.

The inside is bustling with activity, from an 80-foot long Coca Cola bottle in left field, which houses slides for kids, and a 27-foot baseball glove at its spout, to a miniature SBC park, where kids can smack Wiffle balls over the fence. Outside, a statue of Willie Mays is a central meeting spot near the park's main entrance, and another of McCovey overlooks his cove on the Bay side.

Known as Pac Bell Park when it opened, the name changed in 2004 after Texas-based communications company SBC (Southwest Bell Corp.) bought the local phone company, putting some San Franciscans in the awkward position of clamoring for the park's original corporate name. SBC is the first privately financed park in Major League Baseball since Dodger Stadium in 1962.

Pac Bell (now SBC) Park: note the Coke bottle (see page 242) and the park's waterside position.

Right: Aerial View of SBC
Park.
*Photo by: Douglas
Peebles/CORBIS*